# NEW FRONTIER: THE ORIGINS AND DEVELOPMENT OF WEST LONDON

Richard Brown with Andy Shelley and Elizabeth Stafford

Published by Oxford Archaeology, Janus House, Oxford

A CIP catalogue record for this book is available from the British Library

Crossrail Archaeology Publication series designed and series-edited by Jay Carver,
Marit Leenstra and Andrew Briffett

Production and design by Oxford Archaeology Graphics Office

Editing by Anne Dodd

Copy editing by Ian Scott

Front cover: Crossrail at Hanover Square

Typeset by Production Line, Oxford

Printed in the United Kingdom by Henry Ling Limited,
at the Dorset Press, Dorchester, DT1 1HD
an ISO 14001 certified printer

MIX
Paper from
responsible sources
FSC™ C013985

# CONTRIBUTORS

**Principal authors**                           **Richard Brown**
                                                **with Andy Shelley and Elizabeth Stafford**

Contributing author                             Kirsty Smith
Picture research                                Kirsty Smith
Maps and Geographic Information Systems          Gary Jones
Graphics                                        Magdalena Wachnik and Charles Rousseaux
Project manager (OA)                            Richard Brown
Project manager (Ramboll)                       Andy Shelley
Post-excavation manager                         Anne Dodd

# CONTENTS

# FIGURES

# ACKNOWLEDGEMENTS

Oxford Archaeology and Ramboll wish to thank Crossrail Ltd for commissioning this book, and Jay Carver, Crossrail's Lead Archaeologist, for assistance, commentary and guidance. We also wish to thank Jay's archaeological colleagues Marit Leenstra and Iain Williamson. Many other Crossrail employees have provided help during the fieldwork stages.

The authors have relied and drawn heavily on the desktop research and reports of Crossrail's archaeological investigations and excavations. These works were undertaken by Oxford Archaeology/Ramboll, Museum of London Archaeology (MOLA) and Wessex Archaeology, and we acknowledge the contribution made by the many members of staff from these organisations. Most reports have an acknowledgement section; these may be accessed at the Crossrail Website. The excavations were commissioned by Crossrail Ltd or Transport for London and facilitated by their contractors. These were Costain Skanska (Royal Oak Portal and Paddington) McGee at Tottenham Court Road and Bond Street and Costain at Bond Street. Once again, we acknowledge the contribution made by the many members of staff from these organisations.

We gratefully acknowledge the assistance of our colleagues at Oxford Archaeology, in particular Gary Evans, a mainstay of the project. Vix Hughes, Mark Dodds, John Boothroyd and Steve Teague all made important contributions during the fieldwork stages of the work. Ramboll colleagues who have provided valuable help and assistance include Phil Emery, Jacek Gruszczynski, Simon Price and Hilary Quinn.

Our thanks go to Michael Smith from MOLA and Peter Moore from Pre-Construct Archaeology for providing non-Crossrail investigation reports.

We also wish to acknowledge the help received from Helen Fisher at Cadbury Research Library (University of Birmingham) for information on Beatrice Welch and Martin Adams at the Greater London Industrial Archaeology Society (GLIAS). Amongst those who have helped us source or granted permission to use images we acknowledge the help of Rob Poulton at Surrey County Archaeological Unit (part of Surrey County Council), Simon Parfitt at the University of London, Karen Thomas and Andy Chopping from MOLA, Charlotte Matthews from PCA, the social history writer Michelle Higgs, Imogen Plouviez at Harper Collins Publishers, Patrick Mannix at MOTCO, Professor Danielle Shreve at Royal Holloway (University of London), Professor David R. Bridgland at

Durham University, Mark Annand at Bath Spa University, Sara Toso at Mary Evans Picture Library, Jacky Hodgson at University of Sheffield Library, Sara Boys at Dennys Brands, Sophia Brothers from the Science and Society Picture Library, Jovita Callueng from The British Library, Nikki Braunton at Museum of London, Jeremy Smith at London Metropolitan Archives, Raven Amirio and Susan Short at the National Gallery of Canada, Mike Markiewicz at ArenaPAL, Laurence Heyworth at Look and Learn Ltd and Elise Bennett at Warwickshire County Council.

We are particularly grateful to Kim Stabler for reading the draft of this book and providing many helpful thoughts and suggestions.

# FOREWORD

The construction of the tunnels, stations and vent shafts for Crossrail have afforded an opportunity to observe a section across central London at a variety of depths and locations. The archaeology found in the process allows a new set of artefacts to be added to the continuing interpretation of London's remarkable history.

Here Brunel's early locomotive depot jostles with 70,000 year old Bison bones and in Soho 12,000 pickle jars are left as another industry moved on through the ever restless economy of London.

Binding these disparate finds together is the (literally) underlying story of London's geology and geography; the influence of the lost rivers of Westbourne and Tyburn, the contours left after the Ice Age which guided later road builders and William Jessop's Grand Junction canal, followed by Brunel's Great Western Railway, all looking for flat straight routes to and from the west towards the ever growing metropolis.

The development of London beyond the twin historic and ancient cores of the Roman City and the Abbey at Westminster is one of transport and water supply being created from surrounding countryside with small farms and villages from the seventeenth century onwards being overwhelmed by phases of hectic development, very often overtaken by rebuilding to meet changing economic value and fashionable taste.

The routing and construction of Crossrail fits into a well-established pattern of connecting London and it's ever widening catchment. The finds presented here allow the context used to support the promotion, planning and funding of the latest transport project to be understood well beyond the terms of benefit cost ratio and also illustrate how such developments are utilised by passengers and business in ways that soon outstrip the parameters used to judge and justify its construction.

The value of what is revealed here is in its cumulative contribution to London's story and how the very latest technology and construction activity in a dense and complex environment can be coordinated for the wider public benefit.

This book provides a new set of finds and analysis to inform the continuing debate on London's history and its surprises prove that in its scale and complexity there are still so many facts and stories to be told and interpreted to an audience insatiable to know more about where they work, live and visit.

*Graham King is the Head of Strategic Transport, Planning and Public Realm for the City of Westminster*

# CHAPTER 1

# INTRODUCTION

## Crossrail

Crossrail is one of the largest single infrastructure investments ever undertaken in the UK, and was the biggest construction project in Europe at the time this book was being produced. The work started in May 2009

**Fig 1** Crossrail construction at Westbourne Park and Royal Oak Portal

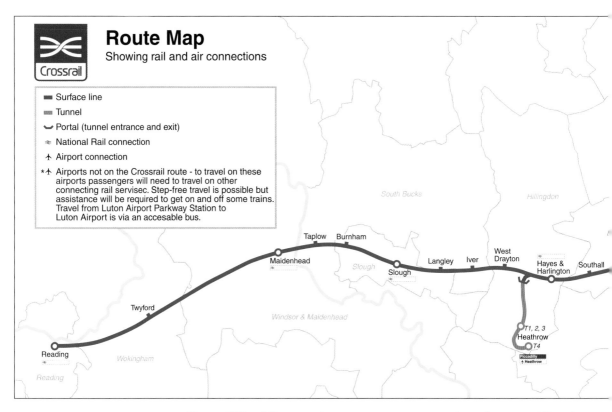

**Fig 2** The route of Crossrail

at Canary Wharf. It comprises new east-west tunnels under central London connecting the Great Western Main Line near Paddington (Fig 1) and the Great Eastern Main Line near Stratford. An eastern branch diverges at Whitechapel, running through Docklands and emerging at Custom House on a disused part of the North London Line, and then under the River Thames to Abbey Wood. Trains will run from Reading and Heathrow in the west to Shenfield and Abbey Wood in the east (Fig 2).

The construction of Crossrail is a formidable engineering achievement. It includes 42 km of new tunnels under London and ten brand new stations, made possible by the organisation of 10,000 people at over 40 construction sites.

When the Metropolitan line, London's first underground, was built in the 1860s it caused widespread chaos and the destruction of many homes (Fig 3). Today, Crossrail is being built in a modern city far more populous than its 19th-century predecessor, avoiding all the existing tunnels and building foundations, and operating within much more exacting 21st-century standards for environmental impact and noise pollution. It has had to minimise disruption to above ground traffic, cater to public interest, and mitigate its impact on the built heritage and archaeological remains. Careful preparation and planning, and efficient communication, has been vital to its success.

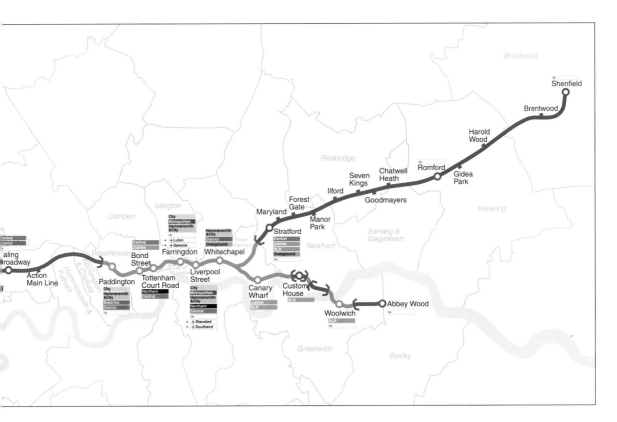

## Crossrail and archaeology

### RESEARCH AND PREPARATION

In the heart of London, it was inevitable that Crossrail would have an impact on archaeological remains and historic places and buildings, and it has resulted in one of the most extensive archaeological projects ever undertaken in the UK. Long before construction began, known and likely sites of archaeological remains were identified in a series of 'route window assessments', which were compiled in 2005 by archaeologists from Museum of London Archaeology (MOLA).

As the design of Crossrail was refined, more detailed site-specific desktop studies were undertaken, carefully considering geology and the levels at which Crossrail tunnels would be constructed. Comprehensive method-ology documents were produced, which included plans for early on-site investigations comprising trenching, test pitting, and the monitoring of pre-construction below ground works such as utility inspections. Figure 4 shows the mapped data for Tottenham Court Road Station and is an excerpt from the methodology strategy. Where these early investigations showed that archaeological remains existed, excavations were incorporated into Crossrail's construction plans. Where there was some doubt about the presence of archaeological remains at a site, archaeological monitoring was scheduled to take place during construction, with contingency plans in place if archaeological remains were discovered. The level of organisation involved has been impressive. As a Project Manager for an archaeological sub-contractor on a single section on the Central London part of Crossrail, the present writer was involved in approximately 12,000 email communications over the period 2010-2014.

**Fig 4** Mapped historic data for the vicinity of Crossrail Tottenham Court Road Station

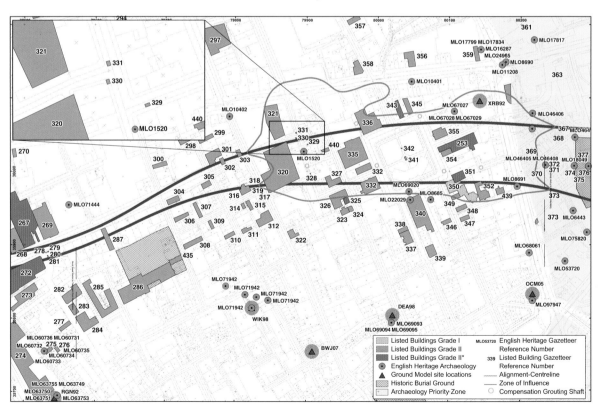

West London lies outside the Roman and medieval city walls and it remained largely undeveloped until the late 17th or early 18th centuries. The first residential squares and streets were laid out in the 17th century, and building work accelerated dramatically during the 18th century. Excavations and observations made during monitoring carried out for Crossrail at Paddington, Bond Street and Tottenham Court Road indicated dense post-medieval remains but a general absence of earlier material. This lack of early evidence may reflect an absence of settlement, but the interpretation needs to be tested when opportunities for further investigation arise. The building-up of West London caused significant below ground impact with landscaping and basement construction, which was preceded by quarrying. The area was later effected by the construction of services, drains and sewers and the building of the underground railways. All these activities will have removed archaeological evidence. Few large excavations have been carried out in West London in modern times and often the archaeological evidence, or lack of it, comes from small 'keyhole' observations during development. The preparatory research work done for the Crossrail project showed that more early evidence does survive in green spaces such as Hyde Park. At Hyde Park, the potential rewards of investigating relatively undisturbed areas with modern archaeological techniques were demonstrated by archaeological investigations in advance of the construction of the Diana Memorial fountain. A sequence of pits, ditches and postholes and artefacts showed occupation of the site during the Mesolithic, in early Iron Age and throughout the Roman period.[1]

**Fig 5** The *Bison to Bedlam* exhibition

## CROSSRAIL RESULTS AND REPORTING

Crossrail has now carried out more than 40 archaeological excavations across the Central London area. In 2012 over 100 finds were displayed in the *Bison to Bedlam* public exhibition, held during July and October 2012 to celebrate the halfway point in the archaeology programme. Over 3,000 people attended the exhibition to see the finds and hear about the discoveries first-hand from members of Crossrail's archaeology team.

A second exhibition, Portals to the Past, was held in February and March 2014 at the Crossrail Visitor Information Centre at Tottenham Court Road. More than 50 archaeological finds were put on display for the first time, including skulls from Roman London, a Roman cremation pot, which still contained cremated remains, flint used 9,000 years by the inhabitants of what is now London, and items found in a suspected Black Death plague burial ground.

For the longer term, results from the Crossrail archaeological investigations are being reported in a variety of different ways. An extensive series of detailed technical reports on the interventions will be available for free download from the Crossrail website. All significant artefacts will be deposited with the Museum of London or the Natural History Museum for Londoners to study and enjoy in the future. In addition, a series of publications will present the project's most important archaeological results, and set them in the wider context of the story of London. This book forms part of that series, and focuses on the Western Central section of Crossrail, where it runs through West London.

### Crossrail in West London

The Western Central London section of Crossrail runs from the boundary of Inner London as far as the City (Fig 6). It provides a transect through West London, an area that remained largely undeveloped until the 17th century and has seen much less archaeological research than the Roman and medieval walled City.

**Fig 6** Detailed maps for the West Central section of the Crossrail route

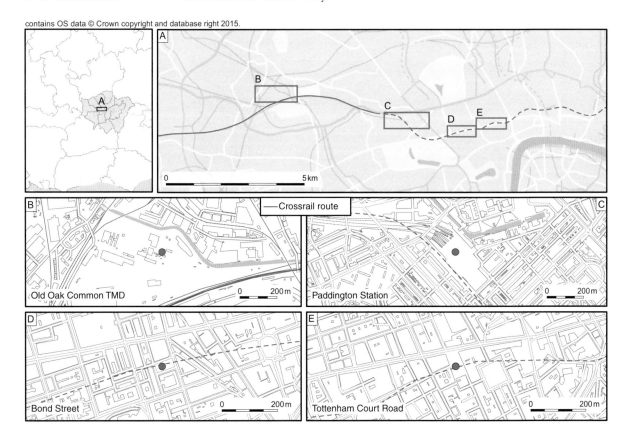

Crossrail's West Central section includes Old Oak Common in the London Borough of Hammersmith and Fulham. Here the sections that form the Crossrail concrete tunnel linings are fabricated. The line continues east, over ground to Royal Oak where the western tunnel portals are located, and then underground to new stations at Paddington, at Bond Street (with Crossrail's new western and eastern ticket halls) and at Tottenham Court Road (also with new western and eastern ticket halls). The below ground works that impact on archaeology at these sites include the station and tunnel excavations but also excavations for grout shafts, air vents and utility diversions. Most of the archaeological work for this section of the line was carried out by archaeologists from Oxford Archaeology-Ramboll UK, a joint venture company created for the Crossrail project.

At Old Oak Common the remains of the world's first fully enclosed railway engine maintenance workshop were recorded, along with subsidiary buildings. At Westbourne Grove, Royal Oak and beneath Lord Hill's Bridge, remnants of Brunel's original Great Western Railway infrastructure were revealed. Monitoring of earthworks at the Crossrail tunnel entrance at Royal Oak Portal, near Paddington Station, located ancient deposits containing animal bones from the last Ice Age, adding to our knowledge of the fauna of that remote period.

Paddington Station is a Grade 1 listed building and records were made of the canopy and railings at the Eastbourne Terrace entrance to the station during their removal and an original wooden sett roadway buried beneath the surface of the present entrance was recorded. The remains of a cobbled ramp, which provided access for horse-drawn carts collecting milk churns from the milk platform (Platform 12) and which was constructed between 1909 and 1916, was also recorded. The excavation of Eastbourne Terrace for the construction of the Crossrail Paddington Station was monitored to track the orientation of the Ice Age deposits, which were recorded at Royal Oak and which extended towards Paddington underneath the historic line of the Westbourne River.

At Crossrail's Bond Street eastern and western ticket halls an excavation revealed the infilled remains of the River Tyburn and the first structures to be built over the river, which comprised 18th-century stables and a well.

The partial remains of St Anselm's Church and School in turn overlay these. Monitoring of utility diversions around the ticket hall construction sites and grout shafts exposed earlier street surfaces and associated features as well as the vaults of Georgian and Victorian buildings under the roads.

To the north of Bond Street, a medieval culvert of mid–13th century date with an early post-medieval brick-vaulted arch roof was recorded by

**Fig 7** Archaeologist surveying the remains of St Anselm's Church in the Crossrail excavations at Bond Street

MOLA in a watching brief during grout shaft works at No. 2 Stratford Place.[2] This is believed to indicate the location of the medieval Great Conduit, which tapped the Tyburn River and supplied medieval London with fresh water.

At the Tottenham Court Road eastern and western ticket halls, the archaeological sequences illustrated the development of the West End, from the exploitation of open countryside for building materials including localised brick-making, to the development of the area's famous streets and squares. During monitoring of utility diversions and grout shafts, a post-medieval brick kiln was found beneath Soho Square. From under the western ticket hall at Tottenham Court Road a large quantity of residual Roman finds was recovered, as well as evidence of post-medieval quarrying and the remains of the original buildings of Soho Fields. Works beneath the eastern ticket hall uncovered the remains of the Crosse and Blackwell factory and warehouse complex. The company were world leaders in modern food packaging techniques. The factory of 19th- and 20th-century date incorporated 17th- and 18th-century structures and its site produced large quantities of historic ceramic containers and product packaging.[3]

Taken as a whole the recorded below ground profiles show how West London has been built up and how it transformed from rural fields to urban metropolis.

**Fig 8** The Crossrail tunnel entrance being formed at Royal Oak Portal

This book aims to use the information gathered for the Crossrail project to illustrate that history, provide an educational resource, and give benefit to the community of West London and beyond. It will also be a celebration of the achievement that is Crossrail, and serve as an introduction to the detailed technical archaeological reports, which will be available online at: www.crossrail.co.uk.

---

## NOTES

1    PCA 2002; PCA 2003, also *The London Archaeologist* **10**, supplement 2, 2003, 60.
2    MOLA 2012
3    See Jeffries *et al.* 2016.

# CHAPTER 2

# LANDSCAPE OF THE ICE AGE IN WEST CENTRAL LONDON

## Introduction

This chapter focuses on the natural history and evidence of human occupation in the vicinity of the Crossrail route through West-Central London during the long period known as the Pleistocene epoch – the Ice Age. The beginning of the Pleistocene is estimated at approximately 2.6 million years ago, and it ended 12,000 years ago at the start of the current warm period known as the Holocene. For hundreds of thousands of years, the climate of Britain witnessed a series of extreme and dramatic shifts, ranging from arctic conditions (glacial periods) when our climate would have been similar to the polar deserts of Alaska and Greenland today, to warmer episodes (interglacials), when balmy conditions prevailed with exotic animals such as elephant, lion, hyena and hippopotamus roaming the landscapes that are today occupied by famous landmarks such as Trafalgar Square.

As the climate swung from cold to hot and back, changes in sea-level due to the waxing and waning of the ice caps had a profound effect on topography, or the shape of the country and its coastline. During the colder periods seawater was locked up in the ice caps, and the sea-level was sometimes as much as 100m lower than today. Huge areas of the North Sea basin were exposed as dry land, creating an immense landmass stretching across Western Europe into Asia. During the warmer periods the ice caps melted, so sea-levels rose and, intermittently, Britain became an island.

It is against this backdrop of landscape change that early human groups such as *Homo heidelbergensis*, and later the Neanderthals, colonised the Thames Valley to exploit the rich hunting grounds. They left stone tools behind them, and these are the most widespread evidence we have today for their presence here hundreds of thousands of years ago. Large numbers of these tools, known to archaeologists as Palaeolithic, or Old Stone Age, have been recovered from the Thames gravel terraces, and were first identified by antiquarian collectors in the 18th and 19th centuries. Many of them are on display at the Museum of London and the Natural History Museum. Although no Palaeolithic artefacts were recovered during the archaeological investigations carried out for Crossrail, the site at Royal

Oak Portal, Paddington, produced a rare collection of animal bone, predominantly reindeer and bison, buried during the last glacial period (the Devensian) beneath metres of sediment and modern buildings.

## Geology, vegetation and fauna (Fig 9)

The River Thames and the City of London lie within a large geological depression known as the London Basin. The basin underlies a large area of south-east England, extending for 250km from the Chalk of the Marlborough Downs in Wiltshire to the North Sea, and it is filled with layers of solidified sediments that were originally laid down in ancient sea beds. The basin was originally formed 40-60 million years ago by the folding and stretching of the earth's crust as the continental plates collided. This event is known as the Alpine orogeny, because it created the Alpine mountain range, and also (on a much smaller scale) the chalk hills of the North and South Downs, the Chilterns, and the Weald. The London Basin is underlain by Chalk and filled by a series of sands and clays,

**Fig 9** Pleistocene geology of the Crossrail route in West Central London Contains British Geological Survey materials © NERC 2014

Contains British Geological Survey materials (c) NERC 2016

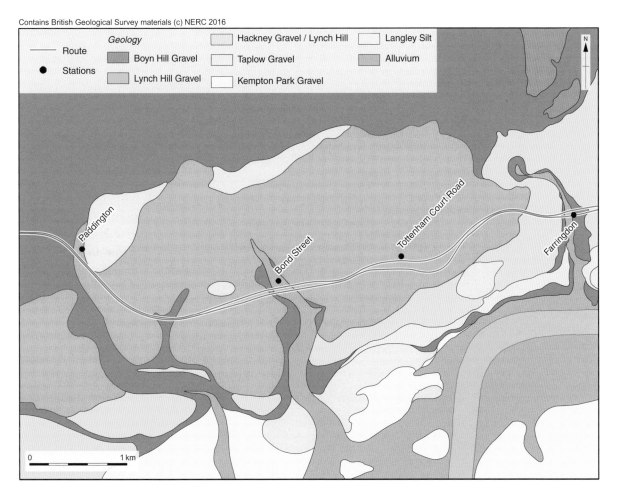

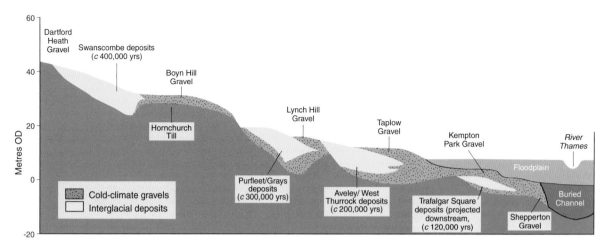

**Fig 10** Schematic diagram of the terraces of the River Thames in the London area, showing the sequence of cold (glacial) and warm (interglacial) sediments and associated sites (after Bridgeland 2006)

mainly deposited in shallow marine and estuarine conditions prior to the Pleistocene. The London Clay Formation, which forms part of this early sequence, is well-known to collectors for containing fossils of tropical or sub-tropical plants and animals indicating that in the remote past this was a habitat of mangrove forests with nipa palms and magnolia bordering a warm, shallow ocean. It was perhaps similar to Indonesia or East Africa today. Fossil fauna include turtles, fish, sharks and molluscs.

Younger sediments dating to the Pleistocene epoch lie above the London Clay, where they have not been eroded by the river or removed by wind action or later disturbances such as quarrying, ploughing and building (Fig 9). These sediments include sands and gravels of old river terraces deposited by the Thames and its tributaries. These terraces have been mapped by the British Geological Survey (Fig 10).[1] In the Westbourne Green and Paddington areas the Crossrail route lies on an area of exposed London Clay, while further east the route lies on the Thames gravels of the Lynch Hill terrace, deposited 350,000-250,000 years ago.

The gravel terraces were usually laid down at times of extreme cold conditions when there were few plants or animals living here. Sandwiched within the terrace sequences, however, are sequences of sands, silts and clays that were laid down by the river during the warmer conditions of the interglacials. At such times there were often abundant plants and animals in the vicinity, and sometimes humans as well, and these warm-period deposits are an important source of information for scientists today. At Trafalgar Square, for example, faunal remains that date to the warm Ipswichian interglacial, about 125,000 years ago, include the characteristic assemblage known as the 'hippo faunas' (Fig 11). Species include hippopotamus, straight tusked elephant, fallow deer, red deer, extinct giant deer, rhinoceros, aurochs, brown bear, wolf, spotted hyena and lion. Mammalian remains from the Thames gravels around Trafalgar Square

WHEN LIONS REALLY CROUCHED WHERE NELSON NOW STANDS: THE TRAFALGAR SQUARE OF 100,000 YEARS AGO, ITS FLORA AND FAUNA AND INTERGLACIAL LANDSCAPE.

**Fig 11** Reconstruction of landscape and fauna during the warm Ipswichian interglacial about 125,000 years ago on the site of Trafalgar Square (Mary Evans/Classic Stock/H. Armstrong Roberts after *Illustrated London News* June 14th 1958)

have been known since the early 1700s, but some of the best sediment exposures were recorded in 1957 during the construction of Uganda House, and in 1958 during foundation work for New Zealand House in Lower Regent Street. Later analyses were also carried out on sediments from sites at Canadian Pacific House and the Tennessee Pancake House on Whitehall. The sediments containing the 'hippo fauna' are largely made up of sands and silts overlain by the main body of the Kempton Park gravel terrace (Fig 12). Fossil plants, pollen and molluscs suggest the presence of a large slow-flowing river in a landscape of dry grassland and oak forest with maple, ash and hazel. Average July temperatures were probably about 4°C higher than southern England today.

**Fig 12** Canine (tusk) of *hippopotamus amphibius* from Trafalgar Square (Photograph: Professor Danielle Shreve, Royal Holloway College)

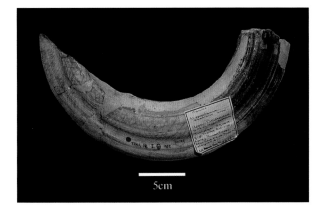

5cm

Further evidence of a later warm interlude, within the last glacial cycle (the Devensian), was found during foundation works for the Ismaili Centre in South Kensington in the 1980s. Temperate plants, vertebrates, molluscs and insects thought to be 60,000–30,000 years old were preserved in channel sediments within the Kempton Park gravel terrace.

In a few areas the gravel terraces are capped with brickearth made up of fine sands and silt and known locally as the Langley Silt Complex. Notable deposits are mapped east of Paddington Station. It is likely that much of the brickearth was initially deposited in the last (Devensian) glacial cycle in a harsh, very cold and dry tundra environment. In such conditions there would have been very little vegetation, making surfaces vulnerable to erosion, particularly by wind action. It is likely much of the brickearth in the London area has at some point been disturbed and redeposited by later river action with further transport and erosion occurring under gravity on areas of sloping ground.

### The Ice Age fauna from Royal Oak Portal, Paddington

On the Crossrail worksite at Royal Oak Portal near Paddington Station, archaeologists investigated a sequence of Pleistocene sediments exposed during construction (Fig 13). The sediments appeared to rest in a hollow within the London Clay on the edge of the valley of the Westbourne, a tributary of the Thames (see below). It is likely that the sediments had accumulated during cold climate conditions, slipping downslope and becoming trapped within the hollow.

An assemblage of around 100 identifiable large mammal bones was recovered; a sizeable sample, especially given the relatively small size of the excavated area (Fig 14). The predominant species were reindeer and bison, now extinct in the British Isles, with the major concentration located in a shallow sequence of channel deposits. The sediments have been dated by the technique called Optically Stimulated Luminescence (OSL) dating, and the richest faunal horizon is 68,000 years old. The bones were studied at the Natural History Museum in London, and the animals seem not to have been hunted, but to have died naturally near the site, where their carcasses were later scavenged by carnivores such as wolves or bears. The chew marks they made on some of the bison bones were examined under a high-powered microscope. The scavengers left the bones behind to be winnowed and transported by flowing water and exposed on the floodplain and banks of the channel, where they were further dispersed and broken by trampling. There was no evidence of human damage, such as cut marks or impacts from marrow processing.

Reindeer are exclusively confined to the 'cold' stages of the Pleistocene in Britain and often occur with bison and cold-adapted megafauna (large animals) such as woolly mammoth, musk oxen and woolly rhinoceros. Reindeer are the characteristic deer of the far north and perfectly adapted

Fig 13 Excavation of Pleistocene deposits revealing animal bones at Royal Oak Portal

Fig 14 Pleistocene faunal remains from Crossrail excavations at Royal Oak Portal. L-R = bison metatarsal, tooth (lower molar) and humerus (Simon Parfitt)

to life in harsh tundra environments. They occur today throughout most of the tundra and taiga of Eurasia and North America. In harsher environments, reindeer migrate southwards from the tundra to overwinter in boreal (sub-arctic) woodlands. These migrations may cover hundreds of kilometres, with herds numbering in the thousands. Other populations make shorter seasonal journeys from alpine meadows to forests, and there are also non-migratory populations that live permanently in boreal woodland. In the summer, reindeer feed mainly on grasses, sedges, herbaceous plants, mosses, and willow

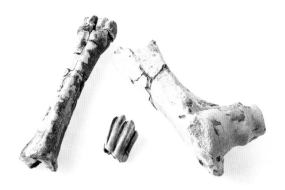

and dwarf birch leaves; in winter their diet is mostly lichens, supplemented by buds and shoots of deciduous trees and scrub. In southern Scandinavia, reindeer survived into the birch deciduous forest stage of the Holocene (about 10,300 years ago), only retreating northwards as the climate warmed, and under competition from other large herbivores.

Bison was one of the most widespread Pleistocene large mammals, occurring throughout Eurasia from at least 500,000 years ago until the end of the last cold stage. It was extremely variable in size and climatic tolerance, subsisting mainly on herbaceous vegetation on grassland and in open woodland. Bison were present in Britain during the warmer periods where there was open grassland but were more common during cold stages in association with steppe-tundra vegetation.

The abundance of bison and reindeer bones at Royal Oak Portal suggests they were the dominant large herbivores. However, the relatively small size of the bison compared to remains from other sites in the region suggests that the vegetation was of relatively low nutritional quality or that the growing season was relatively short. Analysis of the shed reindeer antlers suggests they are from male individuals, and comparison with remains from other sites such as Tattershall Castle and Isleworth indicates similar climatic conditions (warm summers and cold winters) and that the animals were present in southern England at the southern limit of their range during the autumn and winter months.[2]

The site at Royal Oak Portal is of national importance because very few 'bison-reindeer faunas' have been excavated and analysed under scientific conditions. The assemblage derives from a well-defined and understood geological context, with associated dating and environmental evidence.

## London's lost rivers

Although the modern topography of London appears relatively flat to the casual observer, the expanse of urban development masks many subtleties and variations. The dominate feature is the River Thames, flanked by the floodplain zone, now much reclaimed and embanked. Beyond the flood-plain the Pleistocene gravel terraces of the Thames rise gradually like a staircase, the oldest and highest being furthest from the current river (see Fig 10). To the north, a sandy ridge of pre-Pleistocene deposits (the Bagshot Beds) forms higher ground that includes Hampstead Heath and Highgate Hill reaching 134m above sea-level.

The north bank of the current River Thames is dissected by a number of tributaries, but across much of London these watercourses have been culverted - mostly during the 19th century - and are hidden from view.

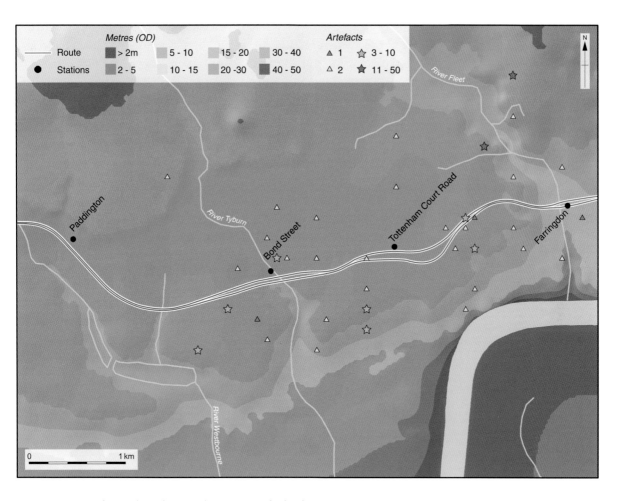

Fig 15 Topography and drainage of the Crossrail route in West Central London and Location of Palaeolithic finds spots. (Contains Ordnance Survey data © Crown copyright and database right 2014)

In West–Central London these tributaries include the Rivers Westbourne, Tyburn and Fleet (Fig 15).

The Westbourne is the most westerly of these watercourses and is traversed by the Crossrail route in the vicinity of Paddington Station. The river flows through the London Clay, and has also eroded a channel in the gravels in Hyde Park. It is one of the more substantial of the northern tributaries, rising from springs on the west side of Hampstead Heath and following a route through Kilburn. At Hyde Park the Westbourne has been dammed to form the Serpentine, before it meanders south, issuing into the Thames at Chelsea Bridge. The Westbourne remained open relatively late and was not completely covered until 1856-7.

The River Tyburn, which also rises on Hampstead Heath, at Shepherd's Well and Belsize Manor, is a much smaller stream than the Westbourne. It flows south through Swiss Cottage down to Regents Park and beneath the grounds of Buckingham Palace. The Crossrail route crosses the Tyburn near Bond Street and its valley is still visible in the present street layout and levels, for example in Mayfair. There is some debate regarding the original course of the Tyburn in its lower reaches because its course was altered in the medieval period to provide a water supply for the city. One theory suggests it may have flowed eastwards towards Westminster, dividing in two to form Thorney Island, where Westminster Abbey was built. Alternatively, it could have flowed directly south from Buckingham Palace to join the Thames near Vauxhall Bridge.

Further east is the Fleet arguably the largest and most important of London's lost rivers. Like the Westbourne and the Tyburn, it rises on Hampstead Heath, from two heads separated by Parliament Hill. The western head forms Hampstead Ponds, and the eastern source the chain of Highgate Ponds. The two sources unite just north of Camden Town, flowing through King's Cross (in places 8 metres below street level) and into the Thames at Blackfriars.

The course of the Thames as we know it today, and the pattern of its tributaries, was established during the Pleistocene. Until around 430,000 years ago the Thames did not flow through London at all, but followed a course to the north-east through East Anglia. It was diverted southwards during the Anglian glaciation (Fig 16); this is an important marker for geologists and archaeologists, because none of the Thames gravel terraces within West-Central London can date before this event. The Anglian glaciation was the most extensive of the last half million years, with ice sheets extending across much of northern Europe. In Britain the ice reached the modern northern outskirts of Greater London at Watford, Finchley and Hornchurch. The advance of the ice blocked the course of the ancient Thames in the Vale of St Albans forcing its diversion southwards into its modern course.

During periods of low sea-level the Thames would have been joined to a vast network of freshwater rivers and lakes across the North Sea Basin and Western Europe. At various times many of these rivers would have drained into a huge lowland river system known as the Channel River system in the area now occupied by the English Channel (Fig 17). When the climate warmed again, the sea flooded the low-lying land and Britain became an island, cut off from the continent.

## Palaeolithic archaeology

Early humans (or 'hominins') of the species Homo heidelbergensis, with their characteristic hand-axes and flint flakes, were early colonisers of Europe around 600-500,000 years ago. So far, only two sites in Britain

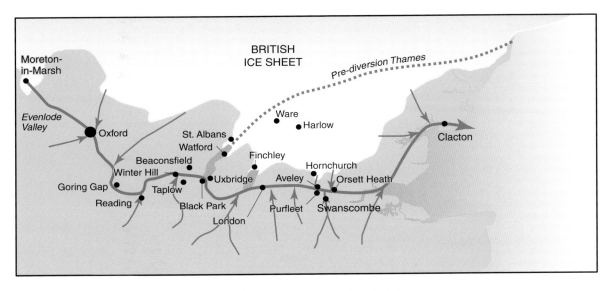

**Fig 16** Map showing the diversion of the River Thames during the Anglian glaciation around 430,000 years ago

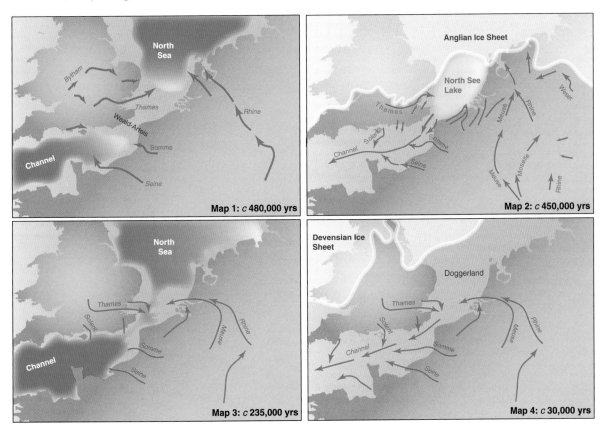

**Fig 17** Palaeogeographic maps of various stages of the Pleistocene illustrating Britain as an island and a peninsula of NW Europe

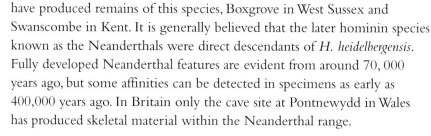

**Fig 18** Palaeolithic stone tools from Hyde Park (after Dewey 1926; with permission of The Society of Antiquaries of London)

have produced remains of this species, Boxgrove in West Sussex and Swanscombe in Kent. It is generally believed that the later hominin species known as the Neanderthals were direct descendants of *H. heidelbergensis*. Fully developed Neanderthal features are evident from around 70,000 years ago, but some affinities can be detected in specimens as early as 400,000 years ago. In Britain only the cave site at Pontnewydd in Wales has produced skeletal material within the Neanderthal range.

Within West-Central London there have been dozens of isolated finds of Palaeolithic flint tools from the Lynch Hill terrace (see Figure 15), although the majority of the tools had probably been moved by the river from their original place of discard. This is apparent from the abraded or worn condition of the artefacts. Many are from antiquarian collections with relatively few recovered in the course of formal archaeological excavation. In 1925, for example, an assemblage of abraded Palaeolithic flint tools (Fig 18), which includes hand-axes and is now in the British Museum, was recovered 950m to the south of the Crossrail route, beside the former course of the River Westbourne, by the Serpentine in Hyde Park. The flint was recovered from a deep trench during repair to the Paddington Sewer and probably derived from the base of the Lynch Hill gravel terrace, about 12m below ground level. At Glasshouse Street, Piccadilly, a small collection of hand-axes now in the Museum of London was recovered in 1913, purportedly from the site of the Regent Palace Hotel. The hand-axe illustrated in Figure 19 is in an excellent state of preservation suggesting it was found close to where it had been left by the last user. It is 17cm long and made from a large pebble of flint, probably collected from the Thames.

**Fig 19** Palaeolithic hand-axe from Regent Palace Hotel, Glasshouse Street, Piccadilly (Museum of London, A11922)

NOTES

1   After Bridgeland 2006
2   Bates *et al.* 2014

# THE COUNTRYSIDE BENEATH LONDON

This chapter reviews the evidence for the landscape of West London from the early post glacial to the medieval period. Much of the history of the area has been, and continues to be, revealed by painstaking recording of archaeological finds, and by research into the available documentary sources.

## Prehistoric West London

The last Ice Age came to an abrupt end around 11,500 years ago, when temperatures rose rapidly marking the beginning of the warm period known as the Holocene that continues down to the present day. Modern humans (*Homo sapiens sapiens*) first seem to have reached England around 40,000-36,000 years ago, and we know that they were living in the Thames Valley during the final cold period of the Pleistocene, around 12,000 years ago. Some of the best evidence has come from a site at Three Ways Wharf, Uxbridge, where the remains of flint tools were found along with the remains of horse, reindeer and other animals that had been hunted for food (Fig 20).[1]

As the climate warmed, trees became established across the landscape and by around 6000 BC a dense woodland canopy covered much of the Thames region, with the river and its tributaries offering important corridors for movement. This period is known as the Mesolithic, or Middle Stone Age. Population numbers were very low indeed, and it has been calculated that there might have been no more than perhaps 1000 people living along the Thames.[2] They were 'hunter-gatherers' with a way of life based on hunting animals and collecting nuts and berries from the wild.

**Fig 20** A reconstruction of a Final Upper Palaeolithic/early Mesolithic camp in the tundra of 11,000 BP (© Surrey County Council Archaeological Unit)

It is very rare to find evidence anywhere for the people who lived here at this time, but Mesolithic worked flints and worked antler have been found at Uxbridge, and are also known from the Lea Valley to the east.[3]

One of the most fundamental changes in human lifestyles took place over the period 4000-3500 BC, when people in our region began to domesticate animals, plant crops and become farmers. This marks the beginning of the Neolithic, or New Stone Age. Neolithic people began clearing the woodland for their crops and animals. They also made and used the first pottery, as well as continuing to make flint tools, and built communal monuments. As with the Mesolithic period, the remains of Neolithic communities are very rare in the region, but it is likely that the attractive river valleys and free-draining soils underlying West London would have been suitable places for occupation and cultivation. Cereal grains of barley, emmer and bread wheat have been found in pits at Curzon Gate, Hyde Park, along with Neolithic pottery known as Peterborough Ware, which dates from around 3300-2900 BC.[4] A Neolithic flint axe-head has been found at Hyde Park corner, and there is evidence of 'ard' (wooden plough) marks at various points adjacent to the Thames at Westminster and elsewhere.[5]

The clearance and division of land for farming in the Thames Valley intensified in the Bronze Age, and particularly in the middle Bronze Age, around 1500 BC. Woodland was felled at this time, and replaced by fields that were managed, maintained and worked by small family-based communities. The River Thames itself seems to have been important to the Bronze Age people of the region, who deposited valuable objects such as daggers, swords and shields in its waters. However, in West London there is only limited evidence for where these people might have lived. A Bronze Age soil horizon with bone and burnt flint was found at Stukely Street, near High Holborn; three poorly-dated hand-axes have been found in New Oxford Street; a possible Middle Bronze Age tool of bronze and wood was found in Great Russell Street, and a flint assemblage was found south of the Serpentine in Hyde Park. Prehistoric and Roman artefacts from the area of Thorney Island, beneath Westminster Abbey (including possible evidence of a quay at Parliament Square), have led to the suggestion of an early river crossing point here.[6] Evidence of a prehistoric trackway has been found at New Oxford Street.[7] The trackway appears to have been used in the Roman period as well.

The Iron Age (800BC –AD50) is characterised by the introduction of iron for tools and weapons in place of copper alloy or bronze. It was also a time of increased trade and migration from Northern Europe, and was characterised by an expanding population and a worsening climate.[8] Many Iron Age finds have been retrieved from the Thames. Frequently these comprise metalwork including swords and daggers, and some of the most impressive finds of this period known in Britain including the Battersea Shield and the Waterloo Helmet. Archaeologists believe that these Iron Age objects were deliberately placed or thrown into the river probably as religious offerings.

However, despite these riches there is very little evidence for settlement in the Greater London area during this period. Iron Age remains located in West London are confined to those recovered on the site of the Diana Memorial fountain in Hyde Park,[9] as well as a coin hoard from St James's Park, worked timbers from Richmond Terrace Mews and pottery from St Margaret Street, Westminster.[10] The area of Greater London seems to have been where the boundaries of a number tribal areas met. Substantial enclosures have been recorded at Ilford (Uphall Camp) and at Wimbledon Common (Caesar's Camp – a name frequently assigned to Iron Age earthworks), and one is currently being investigated at Woolwich. Further possible enclosures at Hadley Wood and Bush Hill Park remain undated.

## Roman West London

London became a much more important place after the Roman Conquest, with the foundation of the City of Londinium following shortly after the invasion, perhaps about AD 50.

The Romans quickly developed an infrastructure of long-distance routes linking Londinium to other towns in the province, and the importance of West London increases from this time as the major roads leading west from the City were established. Watling Street (Edgware Road/Park Lane) ran from Dover to North Wales and Chester; it is thought initially to have crossed the Thames at Westminster and headed north-westwards along the

**Fig 21** The Roman Roads around London

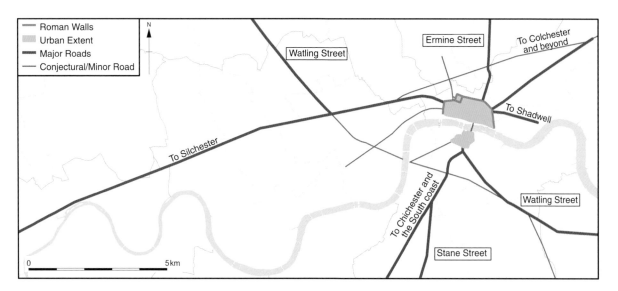

line of the modern Edgware Road and Park Lane. A major east-west highway the 'Via Trinobantia' (High Holborn, Oxford Street and Bayswater Road) ran from Londinium to Calleva Atrebatum (Silchester). These roads ran through an open agricultural landscape characterised by features such as field ditches, gravel quarries for road maintenance and small farmsteads such as that apparently found in Hyde Park on the site of the Diana Memorial Fountain. More permanent occupation might be expected where the roads intersected at the site of Marble Arch, but none

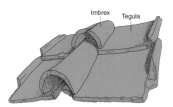

Imbrex    Tegula

**Fig 22** Components of a Roman tiled roof found in Crossrail excavations at Tottenham Court Road

### ROMAN POTTERY FROM TOTTENHAM COURT ROAD

Roman pottery from Tottenham Court Road included pieces imported from the Continent. A Samian ware bowl (Dragendorff form 38), a hemispherical form with a flange around its body, arrived from Gaul during the 2nd or early 3rd century. Samian is finely-made pottery with glossy red surfaces (Fig 23). That it was highly prized in Roman Britain is suggested by examples found elsewhere that bear owners' names or marks or evidence of repair, as well as the many imitations made by British potters. At the same time, Samian was durable and designed for practical use. The bowl present here is of a type that is sometimes heavily worn inside, as if used as a mixing bowl in the kitchen.

**Fig 23** Fragment of a decorated Samian bowl of Roman date from Crossrail excavations at Tottenham Court Road with a reconstruction of the bowl

A handle of a globular amphora (type Dressel 20) was also recovered. This would have contained olive oil exported from southern Spain between the late 1st and 3rd centuries. Olive oil was a valuable and useful commodity in the Roman world, being used not just for cooking, but also cleansing oneself in the baths, and for lighting, and was consequently manufactured and exported in huge quantity.

These are finds that suggest that the people who used the Roman pottery found at Tottenham Court Road were familiar with Mediterranean dining or social practices.

is presently known. There are, however, suggestions of a settlement around Bond Street where the Via Trinobantia would have crossed the Tyburn, probably by means of a bridge (Fig 21).

Immediately outside *Londinium*, and approaching the Fleet River, this road would have been lined with burials and funerary monuments. There are also indications of a Roman masonry building, beneath St Etheldreda's Church in Holborn. The outer limits of the extra-mural cemetery are not known, but individual burials and a tombstone have been found as far west as Tottenham Court.

Roman finds were found on the site of the Crossrail Tottenham Court Road Station during construction. They comprise seven large sherds of pottery including part of a handle from a large olive oil jar or amphora, and a piece of decorated Samian tableware, which date to the early to mid 3rd century. Along with the pottery were thirty pieces of Roman building material including both flat and curved roofing tile (*tegulae* and *imbrices*) and brick (Fig 22). It may be that these Roman finds are rubbish from inside the City dumped along with the later material that fills quarry holes in the area, but the quantity of finds may also hint at some Roman occupation or activity associated with the nearby Roman thoroughfare.

## Anglo-Saxon West London

By the time the Roman army and administration left Britain in the early 5th century Londinium was a city in decline, and it was abandoned almost totally for nearly 200 years. With the arrival of Germanic immigrants from north-west Germany and the Low Countries, known to us as the Anglo-Saxons, the sophisticated Roman military, economic and administrative

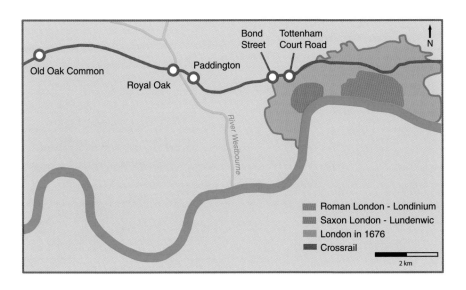

**Fig 24** West Central London in relation to the Roman, Saxon, medieval and early post-medieval city

system with its network of towns was replaced by a much simpler rural-based lifestyle of subsistence farming. Occupation was characterised by scattered rural settlements, whose traces are often exceptionally hard to identify archaeologically. There may have been a number of these in West London. Evidence for 5th- to 7th-century cemeteries has been found at St Martin in the Fields and Covent Garden; an early settlement dating from the late 5th and early 6th centuries with characteristic Anglo-Saxon sunken huts has been found on the north bank of the Thames at Hammersmith, and 6th- and early 7th-century finds have come from further north around the junction of Tottenham Court Road and Euston Road.[11]

The Anglo-Saxons brought with them a new language that formed the basis of the English we speak today. Many of our place names derive from the names used by the Anglo-Saxons to characterise the landscape around them, and to describe their settlements. The place names of West London preserve a memory of its early medieval landscape.[12]

> *Acton* - farm by the oak trees
>
> *Ebury* - island, or well-watered land
>
> *Edgware* - Ecgi's weir or fishing pool
>
> *Hayes* - land overgrown with brushwood
>
> *Holborn* - stream in the hollow
>
> *Kilburn* - royal stream, or cows' stream

and the early medieval people of the region:

> *Ealing* - the people of Gilla
>
> *Harlington* - Hygered's farm
>
> *Harlesden* - Heoruwulf's farm
>
> *Harmondsworth* - Hermod's farm or enclosure
>
> *Harrow-on-the-Hill* - the (heathen) temple or shrine of Gumen's people
>
> *Knightsbridge* - bridge of young men
>
> *Paddington* - Pada's farm
>
> *Tottenham* - Totta's homestead or village

The conversion of the Anglo-Saxons to Christianity began at the end of the 6th century, and shortly afterwards the seat of the Bishop of London was established at the first St Paul's Cathedral. Although much of the old Roman city remained deserted, St Paul's may have been the focus for a new high-status settlement associated with the bishop's seat and church. A new trading settlement developed outside the Roman city to the west from the middle of the 7th century. Known as Lundenwic (see Fig 24), it spread along the Strand and northwards around Aldwych and Covent

Garden. The term *wic* was often used of markets or ports, and the famous early 8th-century Anglo-Saxon writer Bede refers to Lundenwic as an emporium for many people coming by land and sea. The settlement covered over 60 hectares, bordered roughly by modern Trafalgar Square in the west, possibly the Fleet valley to the east and the Thames to the south. It extended at least as far north as Short's Gardens and Macklin Street, the boundary possibly marked in the vicinity of the Crossrail route by the old Roman road (High Holborn). It may be that there was a church at St Martin-in-the-Fields at this time, and also perhaps at St Giles-in-the-Fields, where roads running north from the Strand through Lundenwic met Watling Street.

The Viking raids in the 9th century showed how very vulnerable rich undefended places like *Lundenwic* were, and from AD 886, the old Roman walled city was reoccupied and refortified, under the direction of King Alfred the Great. It became known as Lundenburgh. Lundenwic was abandoned and soon reverted to open ground; its existence was almost entirely forgotten and was preserved only in the name Aldwych (initially ealdwic – old market or trading place) until it was rediscovered through archaeological excavations in the 1980s.

## Medieval West London

The Roman roads across West London remained major routeways in medieval times, and part of the medieval bridge at the crossing point of the Tyburn along Oxford Street has been recorded. There was certainly a settlement here north of the road, around the parish church dedicated to St John the Evangelist. Its churchyard may have extended south of Oxford Street but the area remained rural, reflected in evidence of field ditches near Wigmore Street to the north of Oxford Street, and at Tenterden Street, near Hanover Square. Drury Lane was the principal road from Aldwych and the church of St Clement Danes to Holborn and villages to the north and west such as St Giles and Tottenham Court.

Much of the land in medieval West London was held by Westminster Abbey. There may have been an important church at Westminster associated with a nearby royal settlement from as early as the 7th or 8th century, but Westminster's greatest early patron was King Edward the Confessor, who ruled from 1042 to 1066. He rebuilt Westminster in the new Norman Romanesque style, and endowed it with extensive lands. Edward's abbey appears in the Bayeux Tapestry.

From the 10th century, documentary records become available and we can begin to form a history of the small settlements that would later become the

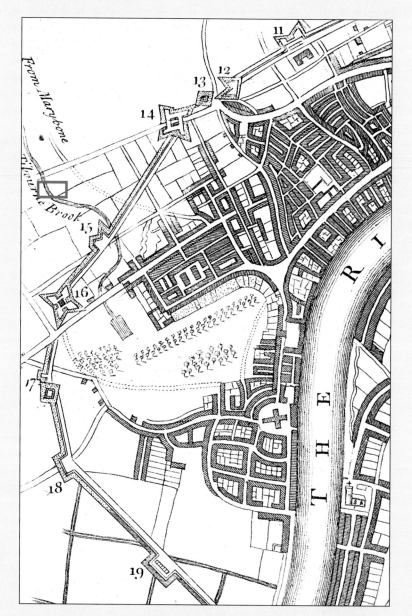

**Fig 25** Map of the course of the River Tyburn (extract from mid 18th-century map depicting Civil War London: Museum of London, Image No. 005848)

From the early medieval period rivers in the area were utilised as sources of relatively clean water for London. In 1236 the authorities of the City of London acquired rights to the freshwater springs near Tyburn and began laying lead piping to convey the water to the City. The pipe terminated at the Great Conduit in Cheapside, which was probably only constructed in about 1245.

During monitoring of the excavation of a grout shaft in Stratford Place to the north of Oxford Street MOLA archaeologists recorded the location of a medieval culvert. The structure is thought to be a water cistern associated with the 13th-century medieval water supply and possibly represents the Conduit Head House nearest to the Lord Mayor's Banqueting House.[13] The Banqueting House was built much later in 1565 (see Chapter 4).

River Tyburn

**Fig 26** The buried course of Tyburn River revealed by a black silt fill exposed during Crossrail excavations at Bond Street

Both the former line of the river and the route of its conduits are visible in the street plan in the vicinity of Crossrail works at Bond Street. South Molton Street and South Molton Lane to the east are orientated northwest – southeast and are clearly not with the majority of street alignments in the area, which are usually at right angles to Oxford Street. This is because the location and direction of the conduit taking water from the Tyburn to the City pre-dates the street layout and influenced the orientation of these two streets. The former line of the river itself was revealed in excavation under the new Bond Street Station and is also visible as a depression in St Anselm's Place (Fig 26).

formed part of the Abbey's late Saxon endowment of 13½ hides at Westminster as recorded in the Domesday Book. A record of the customs of the manor from *c.* 1225 tells us that there were 30 peasant tenants in Knightsbridge and Paddington, each holding up to 20 acres of land. At this time most peasants owed labour services for their land, and the abbey's tenants at Paddington and Knightsbridge had to farm the abbey's lands as well as their own holdings, helping with manuring, ploughing, harrowing, mowing and carting hay. During the early 14th century the abbey held 155 acres of arable land at Paddington. Open fields survived well into the 18th century and are still depicted on John Strype's 1720 Survey of London (see Fig 45).

There were also extensive and valuable woodlands – one of the tenants of Paddington and Knightsbridge *c.* 1225 was Richard the Forester. Timber from the woods of the manor was used for the rebuilding of Westminster Abbey's nave in the 15th century, with 22 cartloads taken in 1460-61 and 42 cartloads in 1478-9. Paddington Wood was still 44 acres in extent in 1647, but most of the woodland seems to have disappeared by the mid 18th century. The villagers probably lived around Paddington Green, where there was a chapel or church of St Nicholas, later rebuilt and

**Fig 27** Extract from the 'Agas' Map of *c.* 1560 showing St Giles in the Fields

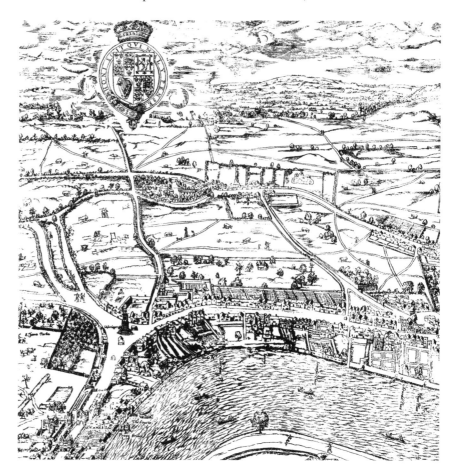

renamed St Mary's. The abbey used the revenue from the manor to support its almonry (its charitable work for the poor), and the Almoner was supposed to make periodic visits to Paddington and may have held manorial courts there.

St Giles at the junction of the Tyburn Road and the road to Tottenham Court, was the site of an extensive leper hospital, founded *c.* 1118 by Henry I's wife Matilda and closed at the Dissolution in 1539.[15] The grounds were enclosed with a wall, and formed almost a triangle, of some 7–8 acres, which is still partly visible as the area defined by St Giles High Street, High Holborn and Oxford Street. The chapel continued as the parish church, and was rebuilt in 1623 and again in 1711. In the medieval period most of the houses belonging to the village stood on the north of the main road from Holborn to Tyburn (now Oxford Street) with gardens extending behind them to St. Blemund's Dyke. The village is almost the only settlement in the area that is generally shown on the earliest maps of London, and it appears in the 'Agas' view as a small group of cottages with garden-plots around the walls of the hospital (Fig 27). In 1541 an Act of Parliament was passed, ordering the 'western road' of London, from 'Holborne Bars' to St. Giles-in-the-Fields, to be paved, 'as far as there was any habitation of both sides of the street.'

## Tyburn, place of execution

From 1571, the infamous place of execution and site of the permanent triangular frame known as the Tyburn Tree (Fig 28), was located near the site of Marble Arch to the west of the River Tyburn. Just southwest of the site of Marble Arch and running south was a tributary of the Westbourne confusingly called the Tyburn Brook.[16] Earlier executions seem to have been carried out close by the Tyburn Brook. The earliest recorded execution is that of William Fitz Osbert, known as William Longbeard, who was hanged in 1196 for fomenting an uprising against Richard I. From the 14th century many political executions took place at Tyburn, including the execution of Roger Mortimer, Earl of March, in 1330. The last person executed at Tyburn was John Austen who was hanged in 1783. Thereafter executions were carried out at Newgate Prison.[17]

The IDLE PRENTICE Executed at Tyburn.

**Fig 28** The Tyburn 'tree'

## Biographical portraits

### WILLIAM FITZ OSBERT (EXECUTED 1196) (Fig 29)

William Fitz Osbert was a charismatic leader who became popular for standing up for the rights of Londoners. In 1195 William became increasingly agitated by rich Londoners evading taxes and began to make inspirational speeches about injustice. He made a visit to King Richard in France to get him to act against the wealthy and improve the lives of the common people. Although the King listened to him, when William returned to London he found that the King's deputy in England, Chief Justicier Hubert Fitz Walter, was unsympathetic to the plight of the poor. William began to rally common Londoners in protests against the rich and he became the leader of a vigilante mob. In 1196 he became a threat to authority and his capture and execution was ordered by Hubert Fitz Walter. He held out for a while by fortifying the church at St Marylebone until Hubert's men set the church on fire. After his capture he was stripped naked and tied to a horse and dragged through the streets of London to be hanged at Tyburn.

The Death of Longbeard.

**Fig 29** Victorian image of the death of William FitzOsbert known as 'Longbeard' (Mary Evans Picture Library, No. 10141829)

William Fitz Osbert is reputedly the first person to have been hanged at Tyburn, although it is likely he was killed by being dragged over the rough and flinty Tyburn Road.[18]

## ROSE TURPIN (DIED C. 1214)

Rose Turpin was a West Londoner who became one of a small number of medieval women to own land and property. She is known from a document charting the donors of land to Westminster Abbey and her profession was cushion maker. She was the wife of William Turpin who was an Officer of the Chamber to King Henry II. In 1177 William Turpin drew up a grant which left Rose his land and property in the event of his death. By 1209 William Turpin had become a monk and Rose Turpin inherited land with its *'stone houses and appurtenances'*. The grant also gave Rose the freedom to choose who she wanted the land to be given to *'Rose can give this to any church she pleases for the souls of herself, of her husband and of King Henry'*. Rose probably died in January 1214 and her lands were donated to Westminster Abbey.

During the medieval period England was a deeply religious Christian society and it was relatively common for wealthy patrons to bestow land and money on religious institutions in return for spiritual services. From late 11th to the 13th century Westminster Abbey sought to consolidate the lands it lost after the destabilising effect of the Norman Conquest. The monks at Westminster went as far as forging or amending charters from donors during this period to increase self-sufficiency and decrease the reliance on royal patronage. Westminster Abbey looked for wealthy benefactors such as Rose Turpin to increase its lands at the same time as increasing its commercial interests in London. By the 12th century Westminster Abbey owned much of West London and it continued its expansion until its lands were seized by King Henry VIII in the 16th century.[19]

## NOTES

1    Lewis with Rackham 2011
2    Hey with Robinson, 2011, 193
3    'Archaeology: The Mesolithic Age', pp 21-28 in Cockburn *et al.* 1969
4    MOLA 1996
5    GLSMR-081134; MOLA 2000, 67

6    *The London Archaeologist* **8**, Supplement 1, 1996, 26.

7    Crossrail 2008, *Tottenham Court Road Station Site Specific Archaeological Detailed Desk-Based Assessment* (CR-SD-TCR-EN-SR-00001)

8    MOLA 2000, 102.

9    PCA 2002, PCA 2003, also *The London Archaeologist* **10**, supplement 2, 2003, 60.

10   Kent 1978, 55-56; MOLA 2000, 117, gazetteer no. WM3; Andrews and Merriman 1986, 17-21; MOLA 2000, 105,117, gazetteer no. WM1; MOLA 2000, 117, gazetteer no. WM2.

11   Cowie and Blackmore 2012, 106

12   Ibid, table 74

13   MOLA 2014

14   The following is based on 'Paddington: Growth, settlement and building to *c*.1800', pp. 181-182 in Baker *et al.* 1989

15   'St Giles-in-the-Fields', pp. 197-206 in Walford 1878

16   Barton 1962, 98

17   'Paddington: Tyburnia', pp. 190-198, in Baker *et al.* 1989

18   Brooke 1975, 45; Keene 2004; Stephen Lewis, 2014, William Longbeard – Popular Agitator or Dangerous Demagogue? URL: The Wild Peak http://thewildpeak.word press.com/tag/william-fitz-osbert/

19   Mason 1996, 172-173; 'Charters of donors: Property outside the walls (nos. 386-99)', 228-241, in Mason 1988; 'Introduction', 1-23, in idem, 1988

# CHAPTER 4

# THE EARLY
# PROPERTY DEVELOPERS

The 16th and 17th centuries saw the character of West London begin to change. At a national level the population was rising fast, and London became ever more dominant as the mercantile, financial, political and cultural capital of the country. It has been estimated that the population of London grew from around 150,000 in 1580 to at least 500,000 by 1660.[1] The City began to spread beyond its medieval limits. The landholdings of the medieval church in West London had largely passed into royal and secular hands, preparing the way for a boom in speculative building. The excavations in the West–Central section of Crossrail have helped to reveal more clearly the story of West London's emergence, illustrated by the presence of brick quarries and kilns as well as the remnants of the buildings of the earliest 'property developments'.

## Henry VIII and the development of Westminster

The royal court and the government had been based at Westminster since the 13th century, but the land around had been granted to the church in the medieval period, and much of West London in the early 16th century was in the hands of religious houses such as Westminster Abbey, Abingdon Abbey, Eton College and the Hospital of St Giles, or great princes of the church such as Cardinal Wolsey, the Archbishop of York.

The reign of Henry VIII, however, was to see an almost unprecedented expansion of royal building, as the king acquired, built and rebuilt palatial accommodation in the new Renaissance spirit on Thames sites from Greenwich to Hampton Court. Much of this building was on land taken from the church, at first by purchase, gift or exchange, but latterly through direct sequestration. Two new royal residences - Whitehall, and St James's Palace - were developed by Henry in Westminster from 1529 onwards. Whitehall had its origins in York Place, the London house of the Archbishops of York, which was substantially extended and redeveloped by Cardinal Wolsey from 1514. In 1529 Wolsey fell from favour and Henry took possession of York Place. During the 1530s Whitehall was extended and extensively rebuilt. It occupied both sides of the road from Charing Cross to Westminster, with the principal royal apartments on the east,

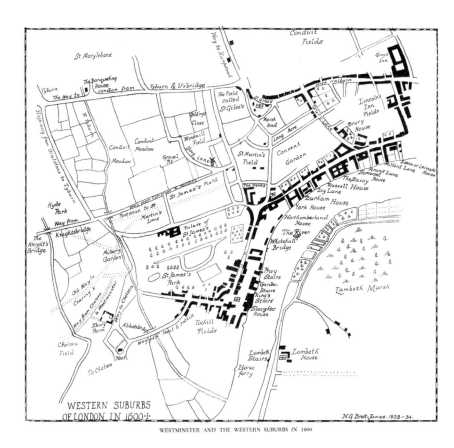

**Fig 30** Westminster and the western suburbs in 1600. (Interpretative plan of West London from Brett-James 1934, 132)

WESTMINSTER AND THE WESTERN SUBURBS IN 1600

between the road and the river, and the land on the west developed into a large royal leisure complex incorporating tennis courts, bowling alleys, a cockpit and a tiltyard. Whitehall was to be the principal London residence of the monarch until it was destroyed by fire in 1698. It was the largest palace complex in Europe with over 1500 rooms. Today, Whitehall retains its role as the centre of government, with state offices lining the street where the rooms of the palace once stood. Only the Banqueting House built in 1622 is still standing (Fig 30).

At the same time as he was developing Whitehall, Henry was also taking possession of the lands of the Hospital of St James, a leper hospital for women dating from at least the mid 12th centur. In the 1520s it held, amongst other possessions, 160 acres of arable land in St James's, 18 acres in Knightsbridge, and land in Chelsea and Fulham. By 1531, the hospital was in the hands of Eton College, and there were only four sisters left in residence. The hospital was suppressed, and Henry secured its lands by exchange with Eton. Henry added further lands by exchange with Westminster Abbey, to form a consolidated block of over 185 acres, part of which he used for the west side of Whitehall Palace, with the remainder becoming the palace and park of St James's.[2] St James's Palace was built in the early 1530s on the site where the hospital itself had stood. It had four courts and a gatehouse. The gatehouse, built in the newly fashionable brick, is the principal Tudor structure surviving at the site today. The substantial stone walls of the hospital were recently revealed by Oxford Archaeology during archaeological work at the palace. In the 16th century, St James's was still relatively quietly situated amid fields, and it may have been intended as a rural retreat. Henry had his new park stocked with game for hunting. Following the destruction of Whitehall by fire in 1698,

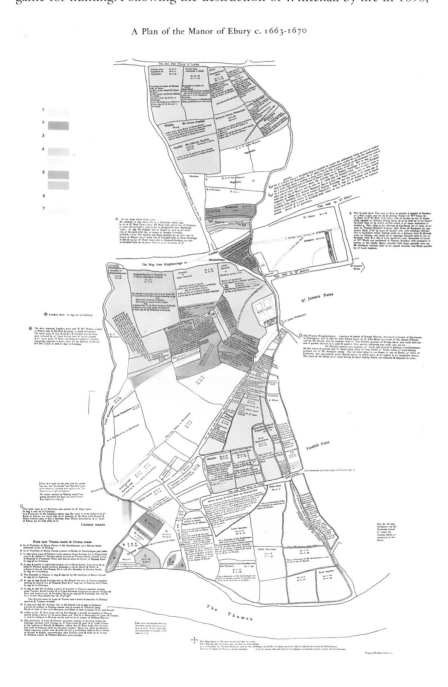

A Plan of the Manor of Ebury c. 1663-1670

**Fig 31** Extract from a plan of the Manor of Ebury in the 17th century with the River Tyburn forming its eastern edge (© British Library)

St James's became the principal London residence of the monarch until 1837 when it was superseded by Buckingham Palace.

In 1536 Henry acquired the manor of Ebury from Westminster Abbey (Fig 31). Much of the land was subsequently leased out, but Henry retained a large area in the north-east of the manor, known as the manor of Hyde, which he enclosed to form a large new royal hunting ground conveniently situated close to his new London palaces. Hyde Park and Kensington Gardens today cover a total area of 253 hectares (or 625 acres). Charles I added a new circular carriage drive known as The Ring, and opened the park to the public in 1637. It subsequently became a very fashionable place to visit. Green Park, an area of 40 acres between Hyde Park and St James's Park, was not acquired by the Crown until 1667-8, when it was bought by Charles II, who surrounded it with a wall and stocked it with deer. It was known as Upper St James's Park, but during the early 18th century it was transformed into a pleasure park and by 1746 was known as Green Park.

## West London in the 16th century

Henry VIII's accumulation of the land that would become West London for his new palaces and parks was mostly achieved with the closure of smaller religious houses, but before the final Dissolution of the greater monasteries. This was not completed until 1540. On 16th January 1540 the Benedictine monastery of Westminster Abbey was dissolved and its properties seized for the Crown along with other church property in the area. The Abbey church, which we know today as Westminster Abbey, was preserved and served for a short period as a new cathedral.

**Fig 32** The Lord Mayor's Banqueting House at Tyburn (Look and Learn History Picture Library)

THE LORD MAYOR'S BANQUETING HOUSE, OXFORD ROAD, IN 1750. (*From Mr. Crace's Collection.*)

Although land ownership in West London was shifting rapidly with the transfer of monastic property, the landscape itself beyond Westminster seems to have been little changed. By the middle of the 16th century the first general views of the City were being produced. A view probably wrongly attributed to Ralph Agas and dating from *c.* 1560, shows West London as a landscape of fields. By this time, Westminster was linked to the City by a continuous ribbon of development, much of it of aristocratic mansions, along Fleet Street and

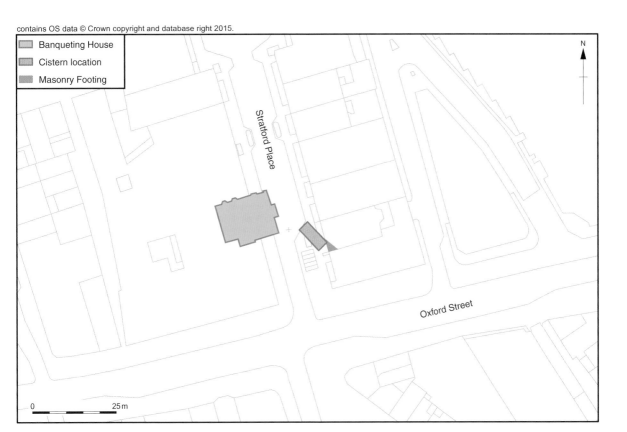

- ▨ Banqueting House
- ▨ Cistern location
- ▨ Masonry Footing

Stratford Place

Oxford Street

N

0    25 m

the Strand. To the north and west St Giles appears in open countryside, although there has clearly been some development along the important routeway of High Holborn and Holborn, leading towards Smithfield.

The City continued to draw clean water from this relatively unpolluted area. In 1553 the Lord Mayor's Banqueting House was built alongside the Tyburn to Oxford Road (Fig 32). It was adjacent to the Tyburn River and served as accommodation for the Lord Mayor and his guests, when he visited to inspect the Tyburn conduit head, which still formed part of the water supply network for London (Fig 33). Although the location of the conduit head is not exactly known, MOLA recorded a masonry structure of Reigate and Kentish Rag stone during the Crossrail works in the light well of No. 2 Stratford Place.[3] Earlier investigations to the north–west in 1979 had recorded a portion of 'cistern wall'. The masonry structure has been interpreted as possibly the footing of the conduit head (Fig 34).

In the early 17th century the construction of engines for pumping water from the Thames, and the consolidation of the City's water supply following the Great Fire of

**Fig 33** Possible location of the Banqueting House and conduit head at Stratford Place

**Fig 34** Masonry structure, possibly part of the conduit head foundation, found beneath No. 2 Stratford Place (after MOLA, 2012, Fig 4)

London in 1666 meant the Tyburn resource was no longer as vital. The Banqueting House gradually fell into disrepair and was finally demolished in 1737.

Rapid population increase in the late 16th and early 17th centuries was accompanied by economic revival throughout the country. Demand for agricultural produce rose along with prices and incomes. The roads that led to the capital were increasingly busy with drovers bringing their 'drifts' of livestock to Smithfield, with packhorses and waggons bringing in valuable wool and cloth and taking away new luxuries such as sugar, tobacco, spices and books for sale in provincial towns, as well as people travelling on foot, on horseback or in coach-waggons. John Taylor's *Carriers Cosmographie* of 1637 describes those who came and where they lodged (Fig 35).

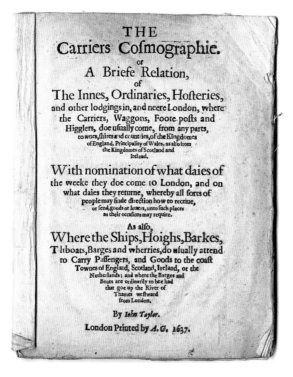

**Fig 35** *The Carriers Cosmographie or a Briefe Relation, of the Innes, Ordinaries, Hostelries,* 1637 (University of Sheffield, Hartlib Papers)

The first passenger stage coaches were running by the 1650s and offered a regular public service. The stage coach made possible relatively safe and speedy transport for travellers, although horseback still remained the common form of transport for those who could afford it, while the less well-off remained on foot. The Royal Mail, which originated in 1516 with the appointment of a 'Master of the Posts' under Henry VIII, was opened to public use in 1635.

New markets developed outside the City walls. The broad street now called Haymarket and connecting Pall Mall with Piccadilly, appears running towards Charing Cross on the *c.* 1560 map attributed to Ralph Agas. When it became a market for the sale of fodder and other farm produce is uncertain, but the first reference to a hay market is in a couplet from Sir John Suckling's *Ballad upon a Wedding* of 1640:

*At Charing Cross, hard by the way*
*Where we (thou knowest) do sell our hay*

The name Haymarket first appears in a ratebook for 1657. In 1663 the Earl of St. Albans, was granted 'a market for all manner of beasts and cattell on Tuesday and Thursday in every weeke in the way commonly called Haymarket Streete.' In 1662 an Act was passed providing for a toll to be charged on every load of hay or straw sold in the streets around St James's Palace including the street 'beginning from the Mews up to Pickadilly' and for the money raised to be used for repairing the road. The market was abolished in 1830 and moved to Cumberland Market near Regent's Park.[4]

WEST LONDON

## West London in the early 17th century

### THE POLITICS OF HOUSING

By the early 17th century there was increasing pressure for more housing. Early 17th-century governments and landlords found it hard to resist the financial advantages of new building, but there was nevertheless a longstanding fear of uncontrolled development, and particularly of the development of poor suburbs that would attract large numbers of displaced rural migrants. The solution was to ensure that the new developments were designed for the rich and respectable, and opportunities began to arise as land in West London gradually concentrated in the hands of the aristocracy, through purchase, inheritance and marriage, and through new grants and licences obtained from the king. The first development, which was to prove an influential model for the future, was the creation of Covent Garden in the 1630s.

Since at least the 12th century Covent Garden had been the 'convent garden', an area of 40 acres owned by Westminster Abbey enclosed by a mud wall thatched with straw. During the 13th and 14th centuries it was a mixture of orchard, arable, meadow and pasture land, with the orchard supplying apples, pears, cherries, plums and nuts for the monks' table, and surplus barley and oats, hay and straw for sale in the market.[5] In 1536 Henry VIII took the land from the Abbey in exchange for property elsewhere, and in 1552 his son Edward VI granted 'le Covent Garden' to John Russell, Earl of Bedford, a royal favourite who had been awarded vast estates at the Dissolution of the Monasteries. The area remained largely open pastureland for the rest of the 16th century, and can be seen on the 'Agas' plan of London of *c.* 1560. The development of Covent Garden from 1631 was the work of John Russell's great grandson, Francis Russell, the 4th Earl. By this time, King Charles I was actively seeking ways of raising revenue without having to ask Parliament to grant taxation. Large sums could be obtained by the issuing of royal licences to favoured individuals to build in London, giving them royal permission to construct new houses despite the numerous government proclamations against new building on undeveloped land. Early in 1631 the Earl paid £2000 into the royal Privy Purse, and was granted the king's licence for *'howses and buildings fitt for the habitac[i]ons of Gentlemen and men of abillity'*. Charles seems to have taken an interest in the designs, as it was later recorded that *'Before the building was upon this licence [erected] the plot of it was showed to his Majesty's view and HM was also graciously pleased to view also the plans in his own person, attended by diverse lords commissioners for buildings, whereupon he so alterred the plot of the buildings that were to be erected that the Earl was by that alteration ...put to £6,000 more charges ...'.*[6] The architect of the new development was Inigo Jones, the Surveyor of the King's Works, who had twice visited Italy and gained first-hand knowledge of the latest Italian architectural styles. Building began almost immediately, and by April 1631 the streets had been marked out. The development was designed as a square, or piazza, in Italian style, two sides of which, were formed of grand terraced houses, with the church of St Paul on the west and the walled gardens of Bedford House on the south. The Earl himself saw to the construction of the church, but generally leased out the house plots to London builders and tradesmen, creating a financial model for development that was later to be widely copied. The houses initially attracted wealthy tenants, but following the establishment of the market, by 1670 the aristocracy moved out, and Covent Garden became an area of coffee houses and taverns and, by the 18th century, a notorious red-light district.

## THE CIVIL WAR

The early impetus of development was interrupted by the Civil War that broke out in 1642. Bitterly fought military campaigns were played out across the country but ultimately came no closer to the Parliamentarian supporting capital than Brentford and Turnham Green. Nevertheless, Londoners had prepared for the possibility. An earthwork and brick bastion circuit of defences was constructed around the City. Crossing the Tyburn

**Fig 36** Mid 18th-century plan of the Civil War defences in *c.* 1643. Although parts of the defences were still surviving when the plan drawn, it is flawed. It is also flawed in its representation of the development of West London, for it shows buildings of St James that were not built in *c.* 1643 (Museum of London, Image Number 005848)

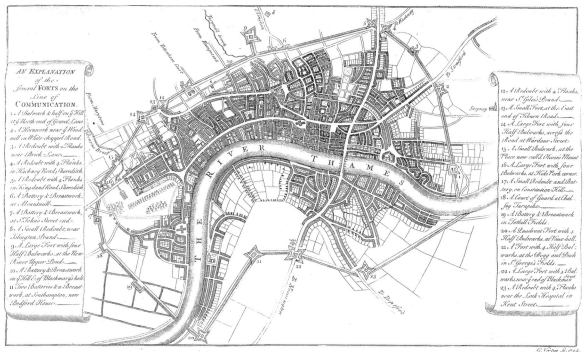

A PLAN of the City and Suburbs of LONDON as fortified by Order of PARLIAMENT in the Years 1642 & 1643.

to Oxford Road near present-day Tottenham Court Road, the circuit continued through what is now the garden of Buckingham Palace and on to the Thames (Fig 36). The defence was short-lived, although some traces of the earthworks were still visible in the 18th century. Recent excavations by Pre-Construct Archaeology at the British Museum have revealed a section of the infilled defensive ditch.

Times of war are also times of opportunity and fortune as well as dramatic misfortune. Land, leases and properties often changed hands; the political rewards of survival as the fortunes of the conflict swung from one side to the other, during the interregnum and its aftermath. For instance, the land on which Buckingham Palace now stands changed ownership with each major turn in the Civil Wars leaving a fiendishly complex title legacy that required an extensive document survey and below ground investigation of historic boundaries to be undertaken by the Crown in order to establish there were no other claims on the property prior to George III establishing it as a royal residence.

## THE RESTORATION

Brett-James' interpretive plan of 1600 (see Fig 30) is a substantially based on a map by Faithorne and Newcourt, possibly initially surveyed in the 1640s and selectively updated.[7] It indicates the growth of West London around the time of the Restoration of Charles II in 1660. Buildings now extended all the way along Holborn to St Giles; the area between Holborn on the north and Fleet Street and the Strand on the south was built up apart from the retained open space in Lincoln's Inn Fields, and Covent Garden is shown. The area is shown in Wenceslas Hollar's bird's eye plan of the West Central District of London, also dating from around the time of the Restoration.

With the restoration of the monarchy, the building up of West London began again. Thomas Wriothesley, 4th Earl of Southampton, had succeeded in not falling foul of either side during the Civil War. The family owned a property known as Blemond's Manor, formerly land of the London Charterhouse, north of Holborn. The manor had been part of extensive grants by Henry VIII to the 1st Earl of Southampton at the time of the Dissolution of the Monasteries. The 4th Earl began the building of South-ampton House in 1657, with a piazza, Southampton (later Bloomsbury, from Blemond) Square to the south. Following the Restoration he leased sections of land around Bloomsbury Square to developers initially on a 42 year lease. Following the lead of Covent Garden, the Earl realised residential areas also needed to have markets and shops. He built up several streets around Bloomsbury Square that were less expensive than the square itself, beginning the idea of providing a mixture of housing types. The writer John Evelyn described Bloomsbury as 'a little town' in his diary of 1665, a description which gives a sense of a self-contained unit.

The grandest of the West London estates was St James's Square, laid out in the 1660s just to the north of St James's Palace. It was developed by Henry Jermyn, 1st Earl of St Albans. The son of a courtier, Henry Jermyn became a favourite of Henrietta Maria, the French wife of King Charles I. When Henrietta Maria's son was restored to the English throne as King Charles II in 1651, she persuaded him to create Henry Jermyn the Earl of St Albans. Between 1661 and 1665, he obtained the land of St James's Field, just to the north of the royal park and palace. His plan seems to have been to create a self-contained court suburb on the model of the Parisian Place Royale, with a market near to the Haymarket (built by 1663), a church, grand houses for the aristocracy around the principal square and streets, and humbler houses for servants, tradespeople and stallholders in subsidiary streets, especially around the market.[8]

The development of St James's took some time to complete (coinciding, notably, with the major plague epidemic of 1665 and the City's disastrous fire in 1666) and the square itself was not built up until the early 1670s. Although some of the houses were built in palatial style, many others were relatively narrow and no better than elsewhere in London. St James's was right at the heart of government and fashionable court life, however, and was highly sought after for courtiers' lodgings. From the late 17th century it became notable as a centre of political life; many coffee houses were established in St James's Street and Pall Mall, and in the 18th century the area became known for its many private clubs (including White's and Boodle's). Henry Jermyn himself lived in St James's Square and died there in 1684.

Henry Jermyn was also to begin the development of another famous London estate, Soho Fields (Fig 37).[9] Here, Henrietta Maria and Charles II had granted him several areas of pasture land south of the main road to

## THE PRE-GEORGIAN ESTATE DEVELOPMENTS

| Parish/Borough | Estate | Started (year) | Finished (year) | Land owner when built |
|---|---|---|---|---|
| Bloomsbury and Fitzrovia | Bloomsbury Square | 1660s | 1660s | 4th Earl of Southampton |
| Soho and St James's | Covent Garden | 1629 | 1637 | Earl of Bedford/Crown |
| Soho and St James's | St James's Square | 1665 | 1677 | Earl of St Albans |
| Soho and St James's | Leicester Square | 1670s | 1670s | 2nd Earl of Leicester |
| Soho and St James's | Soho Square | 1677 | 1691 | Richard Frith & Cadogan Thomas |
| Soho and St James's | Golden Square | 1675 | 1706 | Sir William Pulteney/Crown |

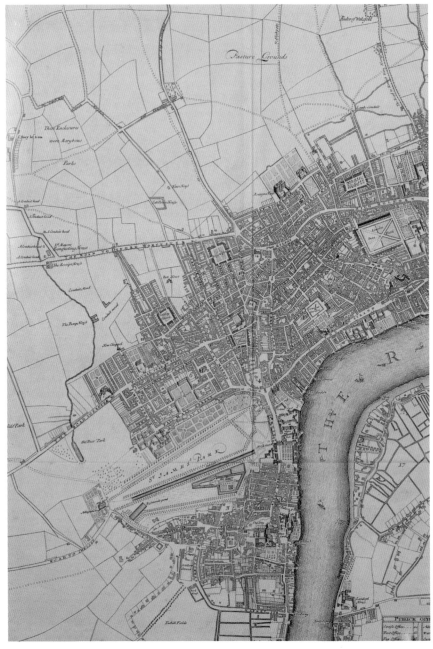

**Fig 37** Extract from Morden and Lea's *'Survey of London, Westminster & Southwark'* of 1700 showing Soho Square and surrounding streets (London Metropolitan Archives)

Oxford, and in 1673 he leased much of the land to Joseph Girle, of St Marylebone who ran brewing and brickmaking businesses. In all Girle paid Henry Jermyn over £2300 for the leases, and in 1676 he obtained a licence to build as many 'houses and buildings on Soho as he saw fit' the only constraint being a requirement to provide adequate drainage for the properties. Girle died the following year, having sold out to the developer Richard Frith for the sum of £4000. Frith had extensive interests in West London developments, and had been involved in building in St James's.

One of the most prestigious contracts obtained by Frith and his partners was to build a large house on the south side of Soho Square for the Duke of Monmouth, the eldest illegitimate son of Charles II. The total expected price for the construction of the house was £7000. Frith and his partners had agreed that it would be built by the end of 1682, but in the event it seems to have been only partly finished when the Duke was there in early 1683. The Duke of Monmouth never enjoyed his property – he was executed for treason in 1685. Soho Square and most of the streets around had been laid out and built by 1691. By 1689 a chapel in Little Chapel Street 'La Patente' had been built for the influx of French Huguenot refugees, who moved to England from 1685; approximately 25,000–40,000 of them settled in Greater London. They needed a place to worship and by 1700 there were at least twelve French churches in the West End of London. By 1694 Monmouth House (which had been standing empty) was also in use as a French chapel.

**Fig 38** Plan of the Crossrail excavations at Fareham Street showing quarry pits (in green) cut by a ditch with adjacent cart tracks. The ditch is later cut by the circular timber-lined cesspit at the centre of the plan

## Crossrail and the building of West London

Much of the building up of West London followed a recurrent pattern. Land came onto the market with the Dissolution of the Monasteries, but

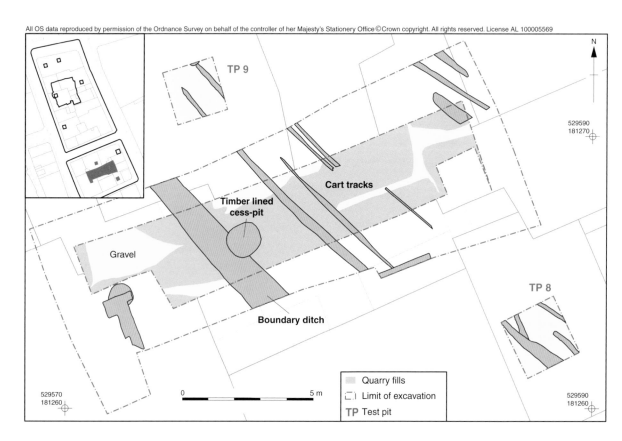

for nearly a century much of it remained farmland and pasture. At a time when travel was increasing along the roads west of the City this became a very valuable source of fodder and grazing land for horses and was often leased out by the Crown and aristocratic landowners. As the building boom took off, land was increasingly being leased out for quarrying and brickfields. Excavations for Crossrail's new station at Tottenham Court Road located quarries of this period beneath Soho Square, Dean Street, Fareham Street and Goslett Yard.

The quarries were subsequently infilled with 'nightsoil' – redeposited from cess pits and domestic waste, including at Fareham Street an assemblage of pottery dating to 1575-1620. This comprised several near-complete drinking jugs in green-glazed Border ware plus two possible candlesticks and two condiment dishes or 'salts'. Border ware was produced at a number of potteries along the Surrey/Hampshire border during the period *c.* 1550-1700, including Farnborough, and was widely traded across southern England. A wide range of kitchen and tablewares were produced. It was valued for its fine white fabric and attractive bright green, yellow or brown glazes and was certainly more desirable than the commonplace redwares produced in the London area. Most households in London at the time would have had a few Border ware pots.

The 'nightsoil' filling the quarries would have been carted out from the City or dumped from the few houses nearby. The tops of the quarries were cut by ditches representing the original laying out of the land plots for this part of Soho and the impressions of cart tracks can be seen running parallel to these boundaries (Fig 38).

The excavations on Fareham Street revealed an *in situ* timber-lined cess-pit (see Figure 38) with discarded pottery, including tankards, jugs, a cup with Chinese style decoration and several fragments of chamber pots, which date from 1680-1710.

The jug and cup are in London tin-glazed ware ('delftware') with blue decoration and illustrate the growing fashion for both Chinese porcelain, still fairly rare and expensive at this date, and tea drinking. The jug is decorated with a popular 'Chinaman among the grasses' design while the cup, or deep tea bowl, carries a pagoda scene. A cylindrical tin-glazed drug jar with simpler geometric decoration would have been used for medicines or cosmetics. One of the two cylindrical tankards is in blue- and purple-glazed Westerwald stoneware, a common German import of the period. The other, in Staffordshire iron-streaked earthenware, is an imitation of contemporary brown English stoneware tankards. The four chamberpots recovered include two complete profiles in Surrey/Hampshire Border ware, and parts of two others in tin-glazed ware and local redware. Dishes

and bowls in these wares were also found. The relatively large number of drinking vessels and chamberpots present in the group is characteristic of deposits of tavern refuse known from London and elsewhere; at the very least it suggests the presence of some sort of establishment where social drinking was commonplace. Eleven pieces of clay pipe, including three pipe bowls of *c.* 1700-1740, were also found in the pit, and tobacco pipes are also a common feature of tavern waste.

Evidence of the brick making industry was found in the north-west corner of Soho Square. Here a spread of compacted brick waste probably represents the remnants of a brick clamp. In the 17th century bricks were commonly fired in one-off brick kilns (or 'clamps') themselves constructed from brick. Once fired the whole structure was then dismantled (Fig 39).

Bricks would be pressed on-site in wooden moulds then stacked to dry. Many thousands of bricks could be fired in one clamp.

**Fig 39** (left) Brick-making waste uncovered in Soho Square during Crossrail works

They would be of variable quality after firing and bricks placed closer to the fire flues became more vitrified and darker. This differential colouring allowed decorative patterns such as diaper work to be laid from the same brick stock.

Although brick clamps have been used from the medieval period to the modern day, surprisingly few have been excavated and reported on.[10] This may be due to the lack of structural elements in the kilns (Fig 40). They are identified by the brick waste material and burning deposits but leave behind little other evidence unless bricks from the last firing were left *in situ*.

**Fig 40** (right) A brick clamp in present day India
(Suyash Dwivedi, CC BY-SA 4.0)

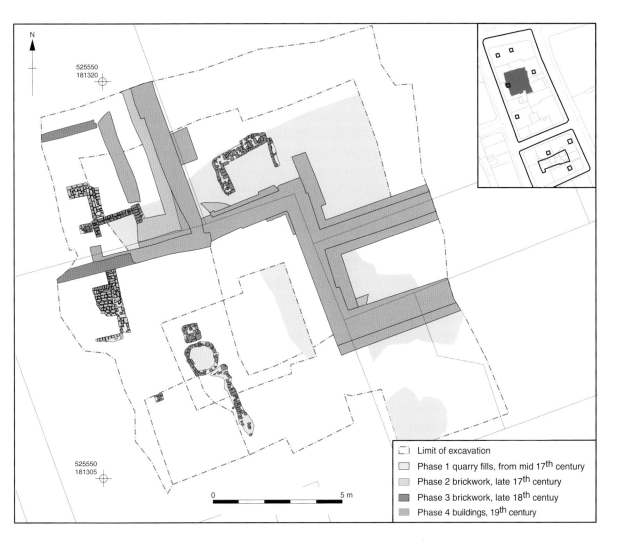

Limit of excavation
☐ Phase 1 quarry fills, from mid 17th century
☐ Phase 2 brickwork, late 17th century
☐ Phase 3 brickwork, late 18th centuy
☐ Phase 4 buildings, 19th century

525550
181320

525550
181305

0          5 m

**Fig 41** Plan of the Crossrail excavations between Dean Street and Great Chapel Street

**Fig 42** Photo of Crossrail excavation at Bond Street showing (1) gravels and quarrying, (2) nightsoil deposits, (3) the first brick building on the site, (4) later cellar walls built below (5) the present street level.

**Fig 43** Extract from a later edition of Morgan's *London &c Surveyed* of 1681-82. This edition probably dates to *c.* 1717 and shows Hanover Square and the surrounding streets and the initial laying out of Cavendish Square (*c.* 1717) (© British Library)

Documentary records suggest that many of the houses of Soho were occupied by the 1690s, but it seems that the standard of building was not very high. Much of the Soho estate was soon rebuilt, particularly from the 1720s, after it passed into the hands of the Dukes of Portland. The Crossrail excavations have uncovered rare evidence for the occupants of demolished early houses. An excavation between Dean Street and Great Chapel Street revealed the remains of one of the first houses built here (Fig 41). The remains comprised part of the building wall and foundation of a substantial fireplace (Fig 42).

By the end of the 17th century, the development of West London was well underway but still piecemeal (Fig 43). The conduited river Tyburn running along Conduit Fields effectively formed the western boundary of the built-up area, and development north of Oxford Street remained very limited between the conduit and Soho Fields.

## Early property developers – biographical portraits

### JOSEPH GIRLE (DIED 1677)

Joseph Girle was a successful 17th-century property developer who not only owned a brewhouse but also owned land and houses in St Marylebone and a property at Westbourne Green. He also used his lands to extract brickearth and provided bricks, often of poor quality, for builders.[11] In 1673 he arranged to lease Soho Fields from Henry Jermyn, Earl of St. Albans, for 53 years starting from July 1677 for which he paid £2333. He also arranged letters patent (planning permission) to build houses there in 1676 but then sold his leasehold to the builder Richard Frith for rent of £300 for the first year and £400 for the subsequent 52 years. He died on 1st November 1677 and Richard Frith paid £4000 to his family for Soho Fields in 1679.

Girle's will of 1675 shows that he and his wife Elizabeth had one son, Joseph, and five daughters. He divided his lands and houses between his daughters and their husbands and bequeathed his brewhouse and associated properties to Elizabeth and Joseph 'for carrying on the brewing trade'. The will indicates that the brewhouse was near the Tyburn Road (now Oxford Street):

> …*my said deare wife Elizabeth Girle for and during the terme of her widowhood …houses where I now live and my brewhouse and field behind the said brewhouse.. and other courthouses and buildings belonging to my said dwelling house and brewhouse and all…houses fronting Tiburne Road.. on the north side thereof and fronting an alley or passage leading from and out of Tiburne Road into the Brewhouse.*[12]

### RICHARD FRITH

Richard Frith was a formidable builder and property developer who was responsible for some of the late 17th-century development of Soho Fields. In 1679 he and the investor William Pym bought the 53 year leasehold for Soho Fields from Joseph Girle's family for £4000. Frith directly managed some of the building work and also subcontracted other builders to construct houses from which he collected rent. He was involved in a number of legal disputes with his tradesmen and creditors and in 1683 he was £60,000 in debt to the estate of Benjamin Hinton. There are no surviving examples of Frith's houses in Soho, due to hasty and piecemeal development and the use of poor quality bricks. Many of his buildings were redeveloped in the early 18th century, but his memory is preserved in the name Frith Street, which has survived into the 21st century.[13]

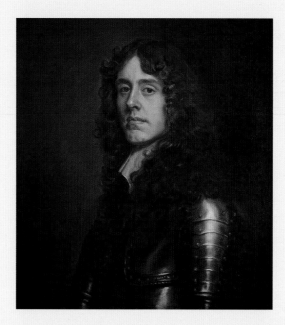

**Fig 44** Duke of Monmouth (Warwick Shire Hall, Warwickshire County Council)

## THE DUKE OF MONMOUTH (1649-1685) (Fig 44)

James Scott was born in Rotterdam in 1649 and was the eldest illegitimate son of Charles II. In 1663 he was brought to England and given the title Duke of Monmouth. In the early 1680s the Duke rented a large piece of land on the south side of Soho Square. He commissioned the builders Richard Frith and Cadogan Thomas to construct him a mansion. Monmouth House was built in 1683 and cost Frith and Thomas over £4000 of which the Duke only paid £1700. Monmouth House was not fully finished and left several people bankrupt because the Duke was beheaded in 1685 for plotting to overthrow King James II.[14]

## NOTES

1    Ross and Clark 2008, 84
2    'Hospitals: St James, Westminster', pp. 542–546 in Page 1909
3    MOLA 2012
4    'The Haymarket', pp. 95–100 in Gater and Hiorns 1940
5    'The Bedford Estate: Covent Garden and the seven acres in Long Acre', pp. 19–21 in Sheppard 1970

6    'The Bedford Estate: From 1627 to 1641', pp. 25–34 in Sheppard 1970

7    *AN EXACT DELINEATION OF THE CITIES OF LONDON AND WESTMINSTER AND THE SUBURBS Thereof, Together Wth. Ye Burrough of SOUTHWARK*, published 1658. Surveyed by Richard Newcourt and engraved by William Faithorne.

8    'General Introduction', pp. 1–19 in Sheppard 1960

9    The following history of Soho is derived largely from Sheppard 1966

10   Eg, excavations by PCA at No. 274 New Cross Road, Lewisham (Ponsford and Jackson 1997, 316–17 and Fig 5) and by Compass Archaeology in North Road, Highgate in the Borough of Haringey (Compass Archaeology 2011).

11   'The Development of Soho Fields', pp. 27–36, in Sheppard 1966

12   Ibid.; National Archives, PROB 11/355/272, Will of Joseph Girle, Brewer of Saint Marylebone, Middlesex (date on the will October 1677)

13   'Frith and Bateman Street: Portland Estate, Frith Street', pp. 151–166 in Sheppard 1966; 'The Development of Soho Fields', pp. 27–36 in Idem 1966

14   'Soho Square Area: Portland Estate, Monmouth House', pp. 107–113 in Idem, 1966

# CHAPTER 5

# THE GEORGIAN AND REGENCY BUILDING BOOM

## Georgian West London

The building up of West London gathered pace in the 18th century as London's population rose, from 674,500 in 1700 to 1,654,944 in 1831.[1] Although mortality rates during the early Georgian period in London were very high and birth rates were low, London's population increased driven by the constant influx of migrants both from within the British Isles and from overseas.[2] This resulted in a young workforce of men and women aged between 14 and 30 years, with relatively fewer children and old people. There were numerous Scots living in London and an Irish colony, known as 'Little Dublin', grew up in St Giles in the Fields. The Welsh in London worked mainly in the livestock industry, including cattle droving and dairying. The number of Jews living mainly in the East End of London in the 18th century is estimated to have been around 20,000. Some 5,000-10,000 black people are thought to have been living in London at this time. Some were slaves or servants, and others were seamen on ships to North America, while Asian sailors called Lascars worked on the ships of the East India Company. There was also a sizeable population of French Huguenots, who had fled to England in the late 17th century to avoid religious persecution.[3]

By 1720, when John Strype published his updated version of Stow's 1598 *Survey of London*, the housing developments of London's aristocratic and speculative builders were filling up the land between the Oxford Road and Piccadilly. Westwards of Lincoln's Inn Fields, the distinctive Seven Dials development had been constructed by 1694, with Covent Garden to the south and Soho, Leicester Square and Golden Square developments of the 1670s and 1680s, to the west.

In 1720, the built-up area stopped at New Bond Street, just past the newly constructed Hanover Square, built by the Earl of Scarborough and named in honour of the accession of the Elector of Hanover as King George I in 1714. The land beyond was labelled 'Pasture Ground'. On the north, Strype shows a sizeable area of new housing around what was to become Cavendish Square, developed by Edward Harley, 2nd Earl of Oxford. In fact the development was never built as Strype shows it (Fig 45), and his depiction appears to be based on the plan drawn up for

Harley in 1719 by his surveyor, John Prince, with a grand open square, church and market.[4] The square was laid out in 1720, but the development was then delayed by economic recession and war, and was built up in a piecemeal fashion over the course of the century. In 1741 the estate passed by marriage to the Duke of Portland.

West of New Bond Street, a large estate that had formerly been part of the manor of Ebury had passed by marriage to a Cheshire gentry family called Grosvenor in 1677, but it was not until to be 1720 that they began to

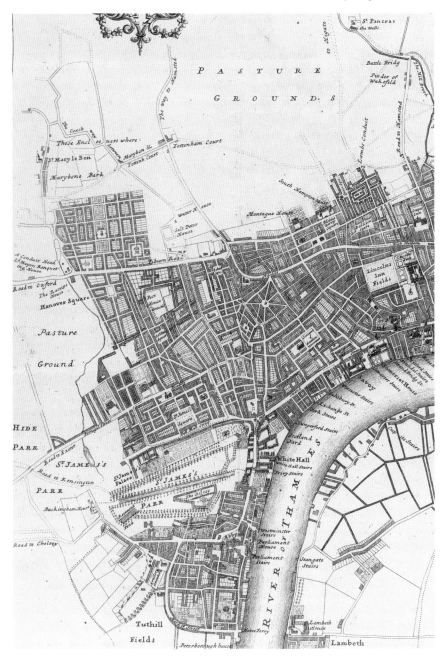

**Fig 45** Extract from John Strype's *A Survey of the Cities of London and Westminster'* (© MOTCO)

develop the estate.[5] The development, which comprised a very regular rectilinear layout of streets around the large central Grosvenor Square built between 1725 and 1731, was built rapidly until the 1740s and remained incomplete for a number of years thereafter.[6] Well into the 18th century the land immediately south of the western end of Oxford Road ('Tiburn Street') was still undeveloped, and builders were reluctant to take leases here because of the continuation of public executions at Tyburn and the large crowds who attended them.

South of the Grosvenor development, and on a distinctively different alignment, is Berkeley Square. The streets of the Berkeley estate are aligned on Piccadilly, where John, Lord Berkeley of Stratton, had built Berkeley House by 1673. The house was bought by the Duke of Devonshire in 1697, but a condition of the sale was that the view to the north was to be kept open. When the estate was developed in the 1730s and 1740s over the former Hay Hill Farm, the square was created on the same axis as the gardens of the Duke's house to honour this agreement.[7]

In the second half of the 18th century Portman Square, Portland Place, Manchester Square and Fitzroy Square were all completed. In many instances developers such as Colonel Fitzroy provided markets (Whitfield Street) and a chapel as amenities for the developments.[8] In 1800 the 5th Duke of Bedford had Southampton House (renamed Bedford House) demolished and created Russell Square. This was followed from the 1820s by the creation of further residential developments on the Bedford estate, including Gordon Square, Tavistock Square, Woburn Square and Torrington Square, all referencing family names and titles.[9]

Transport infrastructure through and around West London was rapidly improving in the second half of the 18th century. Until 1750 London Bridge had been the only direct link between north and south London, but in 1750 Westminster Bridge was opened. In 1756 the first part of a toll road, the New Road, bypassing West London and the City was opened. It comprised three sections: Marylebone Road, which ran from Paddington eastwards through Marylebone; Euston Road, running north-east to Gray's Inn Road; and Pentonville Road to Islington. The construction of the road meant that coach users could expect faster journey times and drovers could move animals to Smithfield more quickly. It also prevented the smaller streets in the area from getting clogged up with traffic.[10] The first experimental mail coach service organised by John Palmer ran from Bristol to London in 1784. It was successful and very soon a network of mail coach services between London and the provincial centres was established. John Palmer was appointed Surveyor and Comptroller General of the Post Office in 1786.

The late 18th century was a peak period for canal construction, driven by the Industrial Revolution and the need to transport heavy goods in large quantities, particularly from the new industrial areas of the Midlands and the North. London was initially connected to the developing national canal network by way of the Thames and the Oxford Canal, which opened 1790. However because of the poor condition of the Upper Thames, a better alternative route was soon under development. The Grand Junction Canal was opened for most of its length by 1800 and ran from a London terminus at Brentford northwards to the canal network of Birmingham, bypassing the Thames almost completely. A branch to Paddington was completed in 1801 and terminated in a basin surrounded by wharves, a hay and straw market, sheds for warehousing and pens for livestock. It became a busy inland trans-shipment point.[11]

The importance of the Grand Junction Basin at Paddington was enhanced with the construction of the Regent's Canal, between 1804 and 1812. This extended the canal route around the north side of London to meet the Thames east of the City at what is now Limehouse Basin. The extension of the canal meant that goods from all over the country could be brought directly into numerous canal basins built around London, but much of its trade would to be lost to the railways within only a couple of decades (Chapter 6).

Edward Mogg's map of London in 1806 shows the extent of development by the start of the 19th century (Fig 46). The new developments of Somers Town and Pentonville lay alongside the New Road. Tottenham Court

**Fig 46** Edward Mogg's Map of London 1806 (Museum of London Image Number 002733)

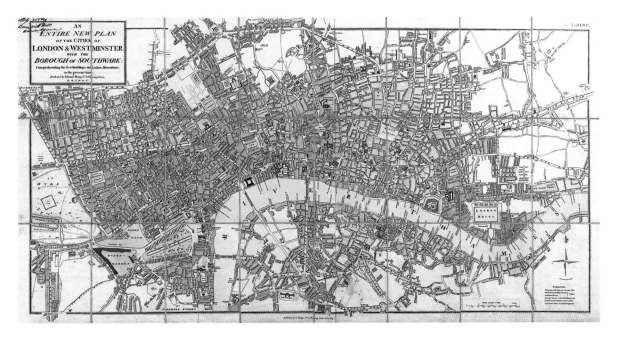

Road has been built up as far as the New Road, with Bedford Square to the east and Fitzrovia (after Fitzroy Square) to the west. The Cavendish estate, now the Portland Estate, had been completed, and the Portman Estate to the west was spreading towards the Edgware Road. The New Road, joining the villages of St Marylebone, Paddington, St Pancras and Islington, was the boundary of the built-up area and remained London's northern boundary until the end of the 18th century.

## Regency and later West London

The Regency period (from 1811-1823) is physically evoked by the construction of Regent Street and Regent's Park. The imposing and distinguished buildings and terraces were designed by Cockerall, Nash and Soane and effectively divided the West End in two, with elite Mayfair to the west and artisan Soho to the east.

The unstoppable outward march of urban development in London is satirised in George Cruikshank's 1829 cartoon showing the development of Camden Town. The trees in the cartoon are saying 'Our fences I fear will be no defence against these barbarians who threaten to destroy us in all manor (sic) of ways'.[12] The cartoon shows the digging of fields for brick earth and the production of bricks in brick clamps (see previous chapter).

By 1850 the ground contained between the City and Hyde Park and St James Park was nearly fully developed and the building industry began to

**Fig 47** George Cruikshank's *London Going Out of Town*. Note the brick kilns and also the predominantly blue slate roofing. A visually striking change that occurred in the late 18th century as the roofscape of West London changed colour, with red ceramic roof tiles giving way to the blue/grey of transported Welsh slate (© Bristol University)

LONDON going out of Town. — or — The March of Bricks & Mortar.

Designed Etched & Published by George Cruikshank. — November 1st 1829

slow down. As the urban development continued westwards and north-wards of Oxford Street so did the industries supporting it. The main industries were based on the construction economy and included brick pits, gravel works, brick and tile kilns, and accommodation for the builders and labourers who were creating the new roads and estates. The periphery of the built up areas also attracted a large number of trades people, such as market gardeners, keepers of dairy herds, tanners and candle makers, alongside a floating population of carters, rag-pickers, bone-boilers, night-soil collectors, washerwomen and horse-dealers.[13]

## Crossrail and Georgian West London

Many Georgian houses survive in West London, and some largely intact streets can be seen, for example at Bedford Place. Often, though, commercial pressures have resulted in the widespread replacement of the original Georgian terraces by more modern buildings. During the Crossrail excavations, however, archaeologists found the surviving underground remains of the Georgian building boom everywhere excavations took place.

As is ever true, the economics of house building on restricted, valuable plots encouraged the maximisation of space on small footprints. Apart from the social elite who could afford to build and occupy detached mansions, most people lived in tall narrow terraced houses. Georgian terraced houses were built on several different levels, with the garden or court at the back being the 'natural' ground surface while the roadway at the front of the building was built up to a higher level. This meant that the basement level was below the road with steps leading down to it (Fig 48). The basements usually led to a storage vault under the roadway, into which coal could be delivered through a hatch from the road.[14] Many of these coal cellars are now disused, and have been cut off from the properties they were originally attached to, and sealed up.

A good example of this process was revealed during Crossrail works in Gilbert Street (Fig 49). A row of surviving cellars beneath the roadway had survived the demolition of their associated houses, the subsequent construction and demolition of the Hanover Branch School (opened in 1889), and the construction of a 7-storey office block (65 Davies Street) between 1948 and 1950. They have now outlasted that building and the construction of the Crossrail Bond Street Station. Cellars like these were

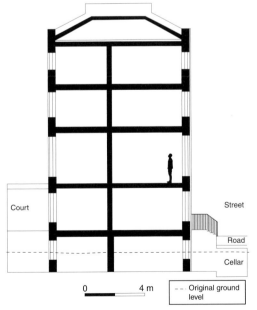

**Fig 48** A typical profile of a Georgian West End terraced house

**Fig 49** (left) Blocked off coal cellars under Gilbert Street

**Fig 50** (right) Cobblestone road surface buried under later surfaces

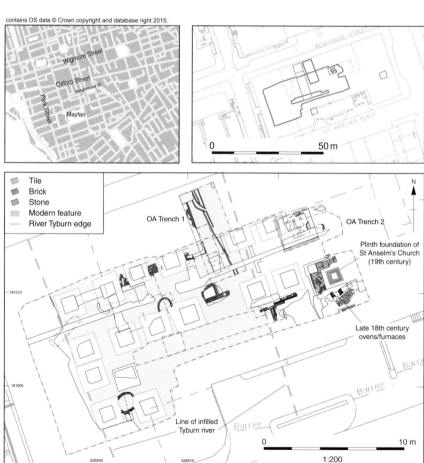

contains OS data © Crown copyright and database right 2015.

**Fig 51** Location plan of the Bond Street excavation

frequently found during archaeological watching briefs around Bond Street and on the Crossrail Tottenham Court Road site in Great Chapel Street and Dean Street.

Crossrail archaeologists also frequently recorded the buried surfaces of London's old roads during monitoring of utilities excavations. These were not datable within the monitoring works as they were usually only seen in the sides of service trenches which were being relocated, but as a general rule in London cobblestone roads (Fig 50) gave way in the 19th century to granite setts, which, although still used, became rarer with the advent of tarmacadam and later asphalt concrete in the 20th century (see Chapter 6 for a note on wooden sett roadways).

## THE RIVER TYBURN

In 1737 a new Bridge was built to replace the medieval bridge over the Tyburn. Conduits had drawn water from the river to supply London since the 13th century (see Chapter 3). Strype's 1720 map still shows the course of the Tyburn running through open land, but Rocque's map in 1746 shows that south of Oxford Street the river line had been lost beneath developments that extend nearly as far west as the Tyburn Gallows (Marble Arch) and Hyde Park. The River Tyburn was investigated and the infilled river was revealed during excavations for the new Crossrail Ticket Hall at Bond Street (Fig 51).

The excavations for Crossrail extended to a depth of 1.5 m into the river fills. Auger samples were taken of deeper sequences and these revealed the clean clays, sands and silts that had formed in the base of the river channel, possibly as the flow slowed due to the extraction of water to supply London. At the top of the sequence was a black organic soil containing artefacts and animal bones, which show that domestic rubbish was being tipped into the river channel in the early 18th century.

A horizontal wooden pipe was found in situ (in a utility trench south of the main excavation) running in a north-south alignment within the line of the river channel. There was also a vertical component consisting of a cylinder of wood with a hole cut through it and an iron handle, which sat inside a wooden pump bucket (Fig 52).[15] These elements are thought to have functioned like a stop cock so that the water flow could be turned on or off at this location.

**Fig 52** Wooden pipe and stop tap components and reconstruction drawing

## WATER AND SANITATION

When the estates of West London were built they had a water supply connected as part of the building programme. In the 18th century water was supplied by the New River Company or Chelsea Waterworks Company. The New River company was incorporated by Royal Charter in 1619, and brought fresh water from Hertfordshire by aqueduct (built 1609-1613) to the New River Head at Clerkenwell. The Chelsea Waterworks Company was established in 1723. The water pressure would not have been enough to push the water above ground level, so it was used to fill cisterns situated at the front of the houses. From here a hand pump was required to raise water into another cistern in the roof space of each house from where it could be distributed throughout the house by gravity. Water supply was intermittent in the Georgian period and was controlled by 'turncocks', who worked for the water companies. The turncocks physically opened and closed sections of the system to manage the supply and make water available to different areas for fixed hours in return for a quarterly rate.[16]

The Georgian builders also constructed channels to take waste water and sewage away from the estates. Toilets called 'bog-houses' were built in the gardens or at the back of the house. These had a brick-lined pit that linked down to the main drain for the house. The main brick drain under each house carried away sewage to the public sewer under the road or to a cesspool in the garden. Rainwater was also channelled away from the roofs in lead pipes that connected to the drains.

**Fig 53** Pearlware from Crossrail archaeological works at Tottenham Court Road

The pits acted as traps for discarded household goods. In one pit excavated at Tottenham Court Road, archaeologists retrieved 377 sherds of pottery including industrialised tablewares from the Staffordshire and Midlands potteries, Creamware and Pearlware with distinctive blue transfer-printed decoration and several fragments of chamberpots. Creamware was developed by Josiah Wedgwood and others in Staffordshire around 1760 and was also made at several other centres across the Midlands and the North, Leeds being one of the major production centres. These refined tablewares were reaching London and further afield soon after this date. In his quest to imitate the pure white quality of Chinese porcelain, Wedgwood also perfected a lighter whiter-looking fabric called Pearlware around 1770 (Fig 53). Pearlware remained popular until around 1840 when an even whiter-bodied fabric was perfected by the Staffordshire potteries. At first Pearlware was hand-painted with mostly blue designs loosely copying imported Chinese porcelain, but from around 1780 onwards it was increasingly decorated with transfer-printed designs which could faithfully (and cheaply) reproduce even the most detailed Chinese originals. By *c.* 1820 blue transfer-printed whiteware pottery was commonplace and

'Willow pattern' was the most popular design found on tablewares throughout the land. The distribution of Staffordshire wares across Britain was aided by the growing network of canals and improved roadways.

Besides tablewares, chamberpots came into general use from the mid 17th century and reflect a growing concern for domestic hygiene and personal comfort. They were made in a variety of glazed local earthenwares. In London they were mostly in common red earthenwares but whiteware chamberpots from the Surrey/Hampshire Border ware potteries were also common, as were chamberpots in tin-glazed ware and imported German stoneware. Wealthier households could afford metal or Chinese porcelain examples. By *c.* 1825 almost every household in London would have had a chamberpot or two in Staffordshire-type whiteware. They are common finds in latrines and cess pits in almost every town and city.

In 1775 a water closet was developed that used a trap to flush water from the bottom of the toilet into the main drain.[17] This type of water supply and waste water infrastructure was only found in the more affluent houses in the Georgian period, but it is worth remarking that Joseph Bramah was manufacturing his patented flushing toilets in his workshop in Denmark Street, St Giles, from 1778.

In addition to the supply of water brought in by water companies, communal pumps were provided and wells were dug in the squares of West London, and reached significant depths, as they needed to puncture the deep layer of London Clay to access water. A well shown on a 1727 illustration of Soho Square was encountered by a Crossrail tunnel boring machine at 30m below ground level (Figs 55-57). The well was a surprise discovery but was rapidly sealed before works continued.

**Fig 54** (a) 1727 illustration of Soho Square, (b) detail of well location (Museum of London Image Number 003207)

**Fig 55** The Soho Square well as revealed in the Crossrail tunnel

**Fig 56** Water from the well in the Crossrail tunnel

Stratford Place structure

Stratford Place

0    25 m

**Fig 57** Plan of the 'Beehive' and associated tunnel

## THE 'BEEHIVE'

An enigmatic underground structure was recorded by MOLA archaeologists at the north end of Stratford Place as part of the London Underground/Transport for London works providing links into the new Crossrail Bond Street Station.[18] The building comprised a Beehive shaped brick vault joined to Stratford House via a vaulted passage (Fig 57).

The 'beehive' is circular, nearly 4 m in diameter, with a *c.* 1.4 m vertical wall from which the vault of the structure springs giving a maximum internal height of *c.* 2.5 m (Fig 58). The structure overlies a brick built sewer (dated to 1772) but did not appear to be linked to it. Some characteristics of the structure and access tunnel suggest that the tunnel may have been added later, and it is possible the beehive was built before the development of Stratford Place. Stratford House is a Grade I listed building erected in 1771-73.

The archaeologists recording the beehive were hesitant to suggest its origins but similarities with ice houses (which were popular in wealthy houses and estates the 18th century) were noted. The structure was supported to prevent any movement during construction works.

## RISING STREET LEVELS

Excavations at both Tottenham Court Road (in Dean Street, Great Chapel Street and Fareham Street ) and Bond Street (Davies Street to Gilbert Street (see Figure 51 above) recorded the very marked build up of the street level during the Georgian and Regency period. Previously streets had been laid on the natural geology – in this instance periglacial brickearths and gravels – which was revealed by topsoil clearance for quarrying/construction. By the end of the Georgian building boom the street levels had risen by up to 3 metres due to the construction of cellars and consequent the raising of road level. In part this was achieved by using excavated material for landscaping rather than carting it away. Later, larger buildings such St Anselm's School, St Anselm's Church and No. 65 Davies Street at the Bond Street completely removed the original back plots, with the construction of their below ground basements.

**Fig 58** The interior of the 'Beehive' (MOLA 2014 Fig 6)

**Fig 59** Crossrail Bond Street excavations showing (1) the infilled River Tyburn, (2) ovens from stables (see Chapter 7), (3) the foundation plinth of St Anselm's Church and (4) the present street level.

## Biographical portraits: people of Georgian West London

### IGNATIUS SANCHO (1729-1780) (Fig 60)

Ignatius Sancho was born in 1729 to African parents; however, sources differ as to whether or not he was born into slavery. A brief biography was written by Joseph Jekyll but there are problems and inconsistencies in Jekyll's account.[19] According to Jekyll he was born on a slave ship, and was baptised by the Bishop of Carthagena. Both his parents died, and when he was two years old his master brought him to England, where he worked for three maiden sisters in Greenwich. It was here that he taught himself to read. He met the Duke and Duchess of Montagu, who took a liking to him and encouraged his education. In 1749, at the age of 20, he worked as butler for Mary Montagu and later as a valet to George Montagu. Whilst in service to the Montagu family he became a music composer and his work was published anonymously.

Ignatius married Ann Osborne in 1758 and together they had six children. He retired from service in 1774 and opened a grocer's shop with his wife at No.19 Charles Street (now King Charles Street), Westminster. He is thought to have been Britain's first black African voter in 1774 and through his writing and inspirational personality helped to advance the cause of the abolition of slavery. His legacy was further enhanced by his letters, which were published in 1782, and his original manuscripts can be seen in the British Library.

### THERESA CORNELYS (1723-1797) (Fig 61)

Theresa Cornelys was born in Vienna in 1723 and became an actress, opera singer and courtesan who in her early life toured Europe under the name Madame de Trenty.[20] In 1759 at the age of 36 she settled in London and called herself Mrs Cornelys, although she was not married. At first, her acting career in London was not a success, however her fortunes changed when she met the wealthy benefactor Elizabeth Chudleigh. In 1760 Elizabeth gave Theresa the money to take over Carlisle House in Soho Square to run a series of entertainments such as dancing, concerts and masquerade balls. Her business became so popular she commissioned several extensions and improvements to Carlisle

**Fig 60** Ignatius Sancho by Thomas Gainsborough (© National Gallery of Canada)

**Fig 61** Theresa Cornelys (Mary Evans Picture Library)

LADY XXXXXXX'S XXXXXXX XXXXXX XXXXXXX XXXXXXXXX XXXXXXXXXX at the XXXX
*The only known portrait of Mrs Cornelys*

House between 1761 and 1772, including a Chinese Room complete with a Thomas Chippendale bridge, costing £5000. From 1772 until the end of her life Theresa's series of failed business ventures got her in trouble with her creditors and the law. She spent her last few years in the Fleet prison and died in 1797 aged 74.

## NOTES

1   Summerson 1945, 9
2   Clive Emsley, Tim Hitchcock and Robert Shoemaker, "London History – A Population History of London", Old Bailey Proceedings Online (www.oldbaileyonline.org, version 7.0, 14 April 2016 )
3   Porter 1994, 132; Clive Emsley, Tim Hitchcock and Robert Shoemaker, "Communities – Huguenot and French London", *Old Bailey Proceedings Online* (www.oldbaileyonline.org, version 7.0, 15 April 2016)
4   City of Westminster 2008, Fig 2 reproduces John Prince's plan of 1719 for Edward Harley's new estate.
5   'The Acquisition of the Estate', pp. 1–5 in Sheppard 1977
6   'The Development of the Estate 1720-1785: Introduction', p. 6 in Sheppard 1977
7   'Berkeley Square, North Side', pp. 64–67 in Sheppard 1980
8   Summerson 1945, 147–148, 156
9   Ibid, 153; Barker and Jackson 1990, 102–03
10  Barker and Jackson 1990, 66–67
11  'Paddington: Economic History', pp. 233–241 in Baker *et al.* 1989
12  Porter 1994, 219
13  Clout 1991, 74
14  Summerson 1945, 49
15  Oxford Archaeology/Gifford 2011, *Archaeology West – Contract No. C254 Archaeological Watching Briefs in the vicinity of Bond Street Stations Event Code XSC10. Interim Statement.* (C254_OXF-A-RGN-C125-50001)
16  'New River Head', pp. 165–184 in Temple 2008; Summerson 1945, 66
17  Summerson 1945, 66
18  MOLA 2014
19  Carey 2003; Joseph Jekyll's *Life of Ignatius Sancho* URL: http://www.brycchancarey.com/sancho/life.htm [accessed: 17 July 2014]; Ignatius Sancho: Writer Musician and Businessman URL: http://www.100greatblackbritons.com/bios/ignatious_sancho.html accessed 17 July 2014
20  'Soho Square Area: Portland Estate, Carlisle House, Soho Square', pp. 73–79 in Sheppard 1966

# THE GATEWAY TO THE WEST: CROSSRAIL AT PADDINGTON

Paddington Station was first opened in 1854 as the London terminus of Brunel's Great Western Railway. Within ten years, it had been connected to the world's first underground railway, the Metropolitan Line, to relieve congestion on the streets of the West End. More than 150 years later it is one of London's busiest transport hubs, with connections to four underground lines, the Bakerloo, the Circle, the District, and the Hammersmith and City, and serves rail passengers from Wales, the West Country and the Thames Valley, as well as Heathrow Airport. Over 34 million journeys pass through Paddington each year.[1]

Crossrail will increase rail capacity in London by around 10% and is expected to carry some 200 million passengers a year. Significant work is

**Fig 62** Crossrail construction at Paddington Station

being undertaken to upgrade existing stations and build new ones to cope with the increase in passenger numbers (Fig 62).[2] At Paddington, Crossrail is building a totally new platform with improved underground access. It is being constructed as an underground box measuring 260m long, 25m wide and 23m deep, and is located directly under the existing Departures Road and Eastbourne Terrace (Fig 63). Construction started in October 2011 and is due to be completed during 2017.

The entirety of Paddington Station is protected by its Grade I Listed Building status. All alterations to its fabric and fittings and all excavations in and around the station for the construction of the new Crossrail station are monitored and recorded by archaeologists under the terms of a Heritage Agreement with Westminster Council. This chapter tells the story of Crossrail's investigations and places them in their historical context.[3]

## The development of Paddington

At the start of the 19th century Paddington was a village on the outskirts of London, but one that was fast becoming a transport hub. It was at the west end of the New Road, constructed in 1757 as London's first northern 'bypass'. Paddington and the countryside along the Oxford Road to the west of London was still attractively rural, but well placed for access to the city, and by the late 18th century there were regular stagecoach services between Paddington and the City.

The opening of the Grand Junction Canal and the completion of the canal basin at Paddington in 1801 (see Chapter 5) had begun to change the character of the area. The construction of the canal had attracted a new population of labourers, and the Paddington basin with its wharves led to a further influx. By 1811 there were 4609 inhabitants, of whom nearly 1000 had arrived in the previous 12 months. The canal also began the break-up of the medieval topography of the parish, isolating Paddington Green from the fields to the north.

A survey drawn by Greenwood in 1827 (Fig 64) shows the Grand Junction and Regent's Canals and also illustrates how Paddington was, by this time, at the western edge of London. The development of the Regent's Canal between 1811 to 1820 had extended the canal route from the basin at

**Fig 64** The future location of Paddington Station on Greenwood's 1827 map of London (Mark Annand/Bath Spa University)

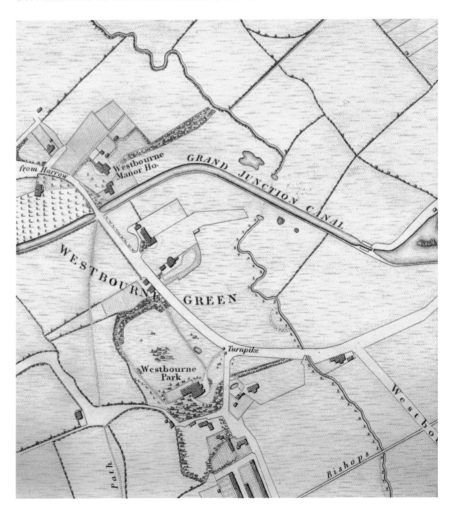

WEST LONDON

Paddington, and skirting Regent's Park to the north, it ran for 9 miles to Limehouse Basin and the Thames in the East End. With extensions to the River Lea goods from all over the country could be brought directly into numerous canal basins built around London. However much of this trade was about to be lost to the railways.

The construction of railways developed from the 1830s onwards, as many private companies were founded to build lines to carry freight between London and England's major ports and industrial areas. Railways were at first restricted to the outskirts of London because of the difficulties of construction in the built-up areas. The first railway in London opened in 1836 running on arches between Bermondsey and Deptford, and was soon extended to London Bridge and Greenwich.

The railways were to have a lasting and substantial impact on West London, with the development of a series of mainline terminus stations on the north edge of the built-up area along the line of the New Road. The first was the London and Birmingham Railway's Euston Station, opened in 1837, closely followed by the Great Western Railway's Paddington Station, which opened temporarily at Bishop's Bridge Road in 1838, and then at Praed Street in 1854. Kings Cross opened in 1851-2

**Fig 65** Paddington Station and locations named in the text

contains OS data © Crown copyright and database right 2015.

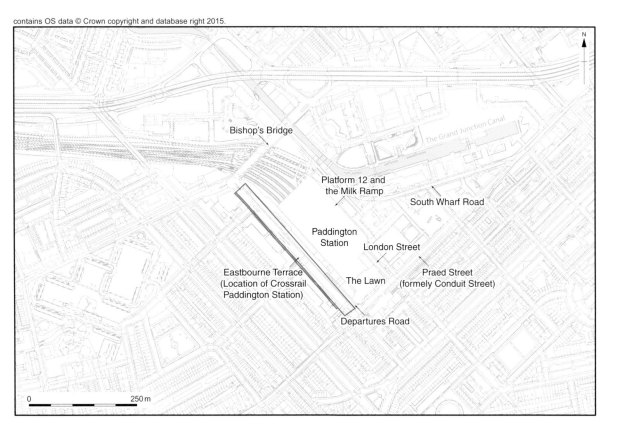

for the Great Northern Railway at the junction of Euston Road and York Way, and was followed by the adjacent St Pancras in 1868 as the terminus for the Midland Railway.

### Paddington: GWR Terminus

The location of Paddington Station as the terminus of the Great Western Railway was chosen by Isambard Kingdom Brunel. His aspiration for the railway was as a trade and passenger service to Bristol and onward to America – a 'Gateway to the West' and the choice of Paddington seems obvious due to its location and the accessibility to the Grand Junction Canal (Fig 65). However the site was confirmed only after much negotiation and deliberation had taken place. One alternative, explored (and abandoned) was for the GWR to share a terminus with the London & Birmingham Railway Company just north of Euston.[4]

The construction of the new station started in 1837 with the excavation of the station cutting and embankments and building of the retaining walls, bridges, drains and roadways. Although the finance was not immediately available to build the intended grand terminus, by 1845 a temporary terminus located within the arches of Bishop's Bridge had been completed. Goods depots and yards were connected by ramps to London Street and Conduit Street to the south-east. To the west of the bridge were the simple timber Departures and Arrivals platforms, turntables, carriage sheds, an

**Fig 66** Modern and original elements of the train shed at the Praed Street end of Paddington station (Photograph: © Peter Cook)

engine shed and workshops. The temporary station was demolished in 1853, and in 1854 the new GWR Paddington Terminus was opened.

The station was designed by Brunel with architect Matthew Digby Wyatt (see insert for a brief biography). The terminus featured a vast train shed 700ft (213m) long covered by three parallel elliptical spans. The design and construction of wrought iron and glass structure were inspired by Joseph Paxton's Crystal Palace, and it was manufactured and built by Fox Henderson and Co, the builders of the Crystal Palace. Over the years much of original wrought iron structure has been replaced with cast iron and subsequently steel (Fig 66). The train shed was a grand and impressive piece of architecture and featured elaborate Moorish styling and colour schemes by Owen Jones (Fig 67).

At the southeast end of the station on Conduit Street (now Praed Street) was the Great Western Royal Hotel, with a concourse known as 'The Lawn'. To the northwest beyond the Bishop's Road Bridge was the goods yard. The station originally had the departures entrance and platform on the south-west accessed by ramps from Conduit Street and Bishop's Bridge Road. The arrivals side was on the north-east side and was accessed by a ramp from London Street. The offices for the Great Western Railway Company were located on the departures side in a two-storey building (now part of MacMillan House).

Crossrail's new Paddington underground station is located beneath Eastbourne Terrace and accessed via Paddington Station's traditional departure frontage. This original frontage, perhaps slightly worn looking in recent years, was designed to be impressive, although the exterior of the building was less ambitious than the interior. Some of the grandeur of the early frontage is apparent in the details recorded by archaeologists during the Crossrail works.

A wooden sett roadway was revealed when Departures Road was excavated.[5] The roadway probably dates from the 1870s rather than being an original feature of the station. It was constructed from deal soaked in creosote and laid on a Portland cement base (Fig 68). The use of wood as a road surface may seem odd to modern eyes accustomed to smooth, relatively inexpensive tarmac or asphalt, but the use of wood as an alternative to more expensive materials such as cobbles or granite setts was seriously considered in the mid 19th century. The first use of wood blocks for paving was in Oxford Street in 1838. In the 1870s the Improved Wood Pavement Company boasted in their advertisements of having laid some 400 miles of paving in the City.

**Fig 67** Decorative ironwork of the Paddington train shed (Photograph: © Robin Sones)

**Fig 68** Diagram showing the construction of a wooden sett roadway (after Boulnois 1895, 61)

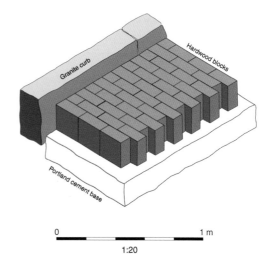

The use of wood seemed a worthwhile experiment, even if it was short-lived and quickly overtaken by tarmacadam and asphalt. The wooden roadway would have eased the ride of passengers and reduced the noise of carriages and horses, providing a smarter entrance to the station for the well-off travellers the company hoped to attract.[6] On the negative side, the life-span of such surfaces in heavy use was only 6-20 years, if turned, and the worn surfaces were shaved, and there were complaints that the wood absorbed horse urine and so wooden surfaces were frequently pungent and malodorous. The almost pristine state of the wood setts when uncovered at Paddington suggests either that the pavement had been well built for durability, or that it had seen only a short period of use.

The Departures Road entrance was covered by the distinctive large glazed canopy constructed originally of ridge and furrow glazing with external

trusses between supporting trough guttering.[7] The canopy rested on piers integrated with the Eastbourne Terrace wall, which was surmounted by ornate iron railings (Fig 69). Gutters channelled water into the canopy supports, which were hollow and acted as downpipes. The south-east end of the canopy featured a gable with a clock and the GWR arms. The canopy was damaged by bombing in the Second World War and now comprises for the most part post-war elements, with only 23 trusses surviving from the original structure (Fig 70).

**Fig 69** Surviving original railings on the Eastbourne Terrace retaining wall (Scott Wilson)

**Fig 70** The Departures Road canopy at Paddington (© Science & Society Picture Library: National Railway Museum Image No. 10326097)

With the opening of the new station at Paddington, Brunel and the GWR's first Superintendent Daniel Gooch moved the whole locomotive department to Westbourne Park.[8] Engines were now housed in a 663ft-long rectangular, brick-built shed constructed to accommodate Brunel's broad-gauge engines. The engine shed housed four tracks spanned with a simple roof of tied wrought iron trusses. The shed was later converted to Stephenson's standard gauge. Lengths of early broad-gauge rails of wrought iron were found at Westbourne Park during Crossrail construction works in 2010, and were identified as the Bridge type designed by Brunel specifically for use on the London–Bristol line (Fig 71). These broad-gauge rails were laid on continuous timber bearers rather than being laid on cross-sleepers as is usual today. Another forms of broad gauge rail used by the GWR was known as Barlow rail of inverted V-shape with broad angled flanges and a concave underside and apparently was intended to be laid directly on the ballast bed without the need of timber bearers.[9]

**Fig 71** Broad Gauge rails found during Crossrail archaeological works at Westbourne Park (© PA Images)

Brunel effectively lost the gauge wars after the Gauge Act of 1846 was passed and in 1861 a new shed was built at Westbourne Park to accommodate standard-gauge engines. The shed was erected to the west of the workshops and originally housed three tracks. In 1873 a further three tracks were added. This building became known as the narrow-gauge shed, with the earlier shed becoming the broad-gauge shed. Another, smaller workshop was located at the western boundary of the site below the Green Lane Bridge. To the south of the GWR mainline lay the Crimea Goods Yard, which housed additional workshops and a coal stage.

## The World's First Underground

The Metropolitan Line, the world's first underground railway, opened in 1863, running from Bishop's Bridge Road just north of Paddington Station to Farringdon Street (now Farringdon). It was so successful that there were soon applications for extensions, and a southern extension to the fashionable districts of Bayswater and Kensington was opened in 1868, with a station at Paddington Praed Street. This was constructed using a cut and cover method resulting in the removal of considerable areas of deposits. Further sub-surface construction work included the building of basements and connections to underground tube platforms. By 1871 Paddington Station was linked to the District Line and by 1884 to the Circle Line.

After the completion of the Circle line in 1884, trains were at first run alternately by its two owners, the Metropolitan and the Metropolitan District or District railway companies. Later District trains ran on the anti-clockwise inner rail and Metropolitan trains ran clockwise on the outer rail. Electric trains were introduced in 1905 by the Metropolitan, which soon afterwards took over the sole working of the 'Inner Circle'. A subway between Praed Street and the terminus was built only in 1887.

By the mid 19th century the Great Western Railway was one of the foremost arteries supplying London, and the opening of the underground Metropolitan Line effectively provided an extension from Paddington Station into London's business district and to a Smithfield Market where the GWR had its own sidings.

### Expansion of Paddington terminus 1908-1915

Paddington has been altered and extended on a number of occasions since 1854. The departures side offices were extended and heightened between 1878 and 1880. Between 1908 and 1915, driven by the need to provide additional track capacity, the station was extended north-eastwards on the Arrivals side with new track beds and fourth span for the train shed. The two new trackbeds housing four lines (numbers 9-12) were constructed beneath London Street. London Street itself was diverted onto a new steel-framed deck (The London Street Deck) built in 1909-12 over platforms 11 and 12. A new fourth span of the train shed was constructed in 1913-15.

The new Platform 12 was set aside for receiving milk and parcels and had a sunken roadway to allow the easy unloading of milk churns from the train, across the platform and onto horse drawn wagons without lifting.[10] Access to and from Platform 12 for milk wagons was provided by a steel framed ramp – known as the milk ramp – which was surfaced with stone setts and channel irons to guide wagons (Fig 72). The milk ramp originally emerged along the north side of London Street at the junction with South Wharf Road. With the increased use of tanks rather churns for transporting milk by the 1930s the milk platform was becoming redundant and finally with the opening of the massive Wood Lane Milk depot in January 1935 it was no longer required and the lines were freed up for use by new suburban passenger services. Although truncated and sealed off, the milk ramp was largely preserved and was recorded before its removal during Crossrail works.[11]

**Fig 72** The surface of Milk Ramp at Paddington

Paddington Station has been as successful as Brunel and Wyatt could have hoped for. More than a century and a half after it was first opened, it still operates day in and day out as originally intended. The new Crossrail station at Paddington is the most ambitious construction here since the creation of the Metropolitan Line. It is being carried out with far less disruption, and no doubt its designers and builders will hope it matches the original station's quality and longevity.

## Biographical Portrait

MATTHEW DIGBY WYATT (1820-1877) (Fig 73)

Matthew Digby Wyatt was born in 1820 and came from a large family of architects and builders.[12] At the age of 16 he started work at the architectural firm of his brother Thomas Henry Wyatt. In 1844 he went on a two year tour of Europe with the writer Henry Cole and when he returned he became not only an architect but also a writer on art history. In the late 1840s Matthew's friend Henry Cole developed an idea for an industrial exhibition in London, which gained the support of Prince Albert. A plan was formed and the Royal Commission for the Exhibition of 1851 was set up, with Matthew Digby Wyatt as secretary. He was Superintendent during the installation phase of the building and he exhibited his architectural drawings during the event.

**Fig 73** Matthew Digby Watt (© The Royal Institute of British Architects)

The Great Exhibition of May to October 1851 in Hyde Park was successful not only in showcasing industry, commerce and art from many nations around the world, but also in housing the exhibition in a revolutionary building made of cast iron with glass panels. The building, designed by Joseph Paxton, became known as 'The Crystal Palace'.

In 1851 the industrialist Isambard Kingdom Brunel was looking for a new design for his railway terminus at Paddington. He was involved in the design phase of Crystal Palace and was impressed with Wyatt's work. He wrote Wyatt a letter about his ideas for the new station:

> 'Now, such a thing will be entirely metal as to all the general forms, arrangement and design; it is a branch of architecture of which I am fond, and, of course believe myself fully competent for; but for the detail of ornamentation I neither have time or knowledge'.[13]

Wyatt went on to design the ornamental ironwork at Paddington Station, his designs clearly influenced by his work on the Crystal Palace.

Matthew Digby Wyatt had a productive life as an architect and was knighted for his work as surveyor for the East India Company. He was Honorary Secretary of the Royal Institute of British Architects from 1855 until 1859 and was awarded their gold medal in 1866. In 1869 he became first holder of the Slade Professorship of Fine Arts at Cambridge University and was awarded an honorary MA.

In 1853, at the age of 33, he married Mary Nicholl (d. 1894) and together they leased Dimlands Castle in the Vale of Glamorgan. Wyatt died in 1877 at Dimlands after a few years of peace from his busy life.[14]

## NOTES

1    http://www.rail.co.uk/rail-news/2013/britain-s-most-popular-stations/; the evidence for the railway heritage of the Crossrail Route, including the development of GWR terminus at Paddington has been considered in more detail in Shelley *et al.* 2106.

2    http://www.railway-technology.com/features/featurecrossrail-paddington-station-london/

3    For a detailed account of the history of Paddington Station see Brindle 2013. The full reports on the Crossrail archaeological and building recording will be available to the public via the Archaeological Data Service.

4    Brindle 2013, 12–16

5    Oxford Archaeology/Ramboll 2015a, *C254 Archaeology West Archaeological Works at Paddington_ XSD10 Eastbourne Terrace Wooden Sett Roadway Characterisation* (C254-OXF-T1-RGN-CRG03-50109 rev3)

6    Information on wooden paving from Clow 2008. See also Turvey 1996

7    Oxford Archaeology/Ramboll 2015b, *Building Recording, Departures Road, Paddington Station* (C254-OXF-T1-RGN-CRG03-50214)

8    The development of the Westbourne Park deport is considered in more detail in Shelley et al. 2016

9    Dow 2014, 125-26, figs 7.3-7.4

10   Matthews 1917, 175

11   Oxford Archaeology/Ramboll, 2015c, *Building Recording: Paddington Station Milk Ramp* (C254-OXF-T1-RGN-CRG03-50215 Rev 2)

12   Banerjee, Jacqueline, 2013, The Wyatt Dynasty, Victorianweb, http://www.victorianweb. org/art/architecture/misc/wyattdyn.html; *Dictionary of Art Historians*, 2014, Wyatt, Matthew Digby (Sir, after 1855), URL: http://www.dictionaryofarthistorians.org/ wyattm.html Date accessed 14 Aug 2014.

13   Gillings 2006, 124 (quote of letter from Brunel to Wyatt in 1851).

14   Waterhouse 2004

# THE INDUSTRY AND ECONOMY OF WEST LONDON

### Food processing

As they speed through Southall Crossrail passengers will catch a glimpse of Noon Product's extensive factory. The UK's market leader in Indian prepared meals was established in 1987 by Gulam Noon, the 'Curry King of Britain'.[1] The business is one in a long line of industrial food manufacturers to have established themselves in west London, many of them along the corridors carved out in the 1830s by the London & Birmingham and Great Western railways. Others include Nestlé, who operate a vast chocolate and coffee factory at Hayes (Fig 74), Horlicks in Slough and United Biscuits in Park Royal, London's largest industrial estate.[2] Despite Guinness and Heinz having left the area in recent years, food manufacturing remains a major employer: Park Royal is said to produce one third of all the food consumed in London.[3]

**Fig 74** Nestlé's factory at Hayes (©Ray Stanton)

It is not surprising that London has a huge food manufacturing base. There are over eight million inhabitants, and nearly a million more flood in each day to work.[4] Geographically, the bulk of capital's national hinterland lies to the north and west, and its excellent transport links made north-west London the obvious location for the production of consumables for the 'home' market (London) and 'export' (the rest of the UK) markets.

Noon was also following tradition in another way. In seeing a market for pre-prepared Indian food he had successfully bet on the willingness of the British to embrace new food products. In this, as in his decision to locate his factory on the outskirts of the city, his business was a late 20th century equivalent of Crosse & Blackwell. This celebrated manufacturer of sauces, chutneys and jams was founded in 1830 when the Soho company of West and Wyatt (whale oilmen with sidelines in curry powder, relish and chutney) was bought by two of its former apprentices, Edmund Crosse and Thomas Blackwell. The pair moved into the manufacture of table sauces, pickles and jams, and quickly found themselves in the vanguard of the industrialisation of food production. They were fortunate to have available the expertise of exiles like Signor Qualliotti, a former chef to

Napoleon who brought with him recipes for piccalilli (Fig 75), potted meat and table sauces.[5]

In 1838 Crosse & Blackwell acquired the former home of Lady Cornelys (see Chapter 5) at 21 Soho Square and converted it into the company's offices and bottling rooms.[6] Gradually, further properties were acquired until by 1865 the company controlled 38,000 square feet of factory and warehouse space in Soho Square and adjacent streets.[7] The volume of production was astonishing; nine million Crosse & Blackwell labels were used in 1864 alone.[8] The Soho warehouses at any one time held 20,000 gallons of ketchup, 6,400 gallons of olive oil and 2,300 gallons of soy sauce.[9] These were prodigious numbers made all the more remarkable because the factory did not possess a railhead, nor access to any nearby railway.

The lack of a railway connection does not appear to have hampered progress, at least initially. In 1877 the company commissioned Robert Roumieu to design a new warehouse for them in the angle between Sutton Street and Crown Street (as Charing Cross Road was then known). Although this was joined in 1893 by a second warehouse, designed by Roumieu's son, on the block of land to the north of Sutton Street (Fig 76), the end of the company's manufacturing presence in the West End was now drawing near. In 1920 the company began to move their production

**Fig 77** Crosse & Blackwell developed a number of other buildings on Charing Cross Road. The building in the foreground dates from 1905 and behind is Robert Roumieu's 1877 warehouse

facilities out of central London, retaining only a rebuilt No 20 Soho Square to serve as their headquarters. The 1877 warehouse re-opened in 1926 as showrooms and offices whilst its northern counterpart was comprehensively redesigned by E A Stone and re-opened in 1927 as the Astoria cinema.[10]

**Fig 78** Archaeological excavations at Crosse and Blackwell's former factory on Charing Cross Road underway in 2010. In the background is Centre Point

The Roumieus' warehouses lay within the perimeter of Crossrail and TfL's cavernous new Tottenham Court Road Station, and therefore had to be removed before construction began (Fig 77). Archaeological excavations on the site duly followed with the aim at improving our understanding of how Crosse & Blackwell had gone about the process of mechanising food production (Fig 78).

Features that had survived the conversion of Robert Roumieu's factory into showrooms and the subsequent demolition included an ash pit beneath a chimney base and the foundation for the factory's boiler (Figs 79–80). A number of brick walls and floors also survived in fragmentary form, allowing it to be noted that the factory's original floor had been of timber planks. This floor was later sealed by a more robust version formed from re-used iron plates resting on timber joists and a levelling layer containing many discarded fragments of the company's late 19th-century glass, ceramic and stoneware containers.[11]

However, by far the most interesting survivor was a concrete-lined brick vault, probably at one time a subterranean cistern within one of the factory's yards. It was found to have been packed with over 12,000

discarded Crosse & Blackwell containers (Fig 81). Most were unused whiteware vessels provided by Maling Pottery of Newcastle, but amongst this treasure trove were stoneware containers known to have been made by Charles Bailey's pottery in Fulham between 1865 and 1890, and quantities of Keiller marmalade jars. Undoubtedly the disposal had been prompted by a move from the use of ceramic vessels to glass containers. There were a number of reasons for this change, chiefly the realisation that glass was inert to most substances and could be washed and sterilised effectively. Glass containers were also more suitable for conveyor belt filling, could be made in a much greater variety of shapes (think of Marmite's jars) and allowed visual examination of the contents.[12]

**Fig 79** (left) Brick-lined pits in Crosse & Blackwell's 1877 warehouse on Charing Cross Road were part of a structure that supported a static steam engine

**Fig 80** (right) Pit forming part of the base of a chimney beside the steam engine base in Crosse & Blackwell's warehouse on Charing Cross Road. The dividing wall was a later addition

**Fig 81** (left) Underground vault uncovered during excavations at Crosse & Blackwell's former warehouse on Charing Cross Road; (right) Part of the vast haul of discarded Crosse & Blackwell containers found in the vault

## Restaurant trade

Although the junction of Oxford Street and Tottenham Court Road is the only place within Soho where Crossrail will have a station, the arrangement of twin ticket halls means that its reach will be extensive. The vast increase in capacity that the new station will bring is required to handle the 200,000 journeys through the station Crossrail estimates will be made every day by 2018. Soho is changing, as Soho always has, and where once Crosse & Blackwell's workers toiled, new offices for today's computer-powered industries will soon begin rising above the station boxes.

Crosse & Blackwell employed many hundreds of our Victorian forebears in their Soho factories. However, far greater numbers worked in the local lodging and coffee-house keeping trades. In 1897 there were over three thousand 'heads of families' engaged in these occupations in the Soho, St Giles and Strand areas.[13] Others worked in the area's burgeoning restaurant trade. This industry flourished as the popularity of the West End's theatres and music halls grew, a growth which itself had been sparked by a rise in disposable incomes and the coming of the railways. The first Soho restaurants tended to be French and one of the earliest, *Kettners* on Romily Street, will celebrate 150 years of trading in 2017. Other survivors include *Maison Bertaux* (established in 1871) and *L'Escargot*, a relative newcomer having opened its doors only in 1927. Between 1906 and 1907 the *Caterer and Hotel-Keeper* published a seven-part series entitled 'Soho and its Restaurants'. This celebrated the district's profusion of foreign provision shops, restaurants and eateries, and noted a shift from French to Italian catering. In a case study of the Boulogne Restaurant in Gerrard Street, it remarked how the proprietor, Mr Ucceli, had found a niche in the market by offering French cuisine at bargain prices.[14]

## Coffee bars and culture

London's traditional coffee houses, which had languished for years, were revived in the early 1950s when Soho become synonymous with a new expresso bar culture (Fig 82), the birth of which is generally credited to a visiting Italian, Pino Riservato. Struck by the awfulness of British coffee, the Milanese dental technician started importing Gaggia's recently-invented expresso machines.[15] In the basement of his shop at 10 Dean Street he opened the *Riservato*, the centrepiece of which was a Gaggia machine. The idea proved popular and in 1953 The *Moka Bar* on Frith Street became the first independent establishment to adopt his equipment.[16]

The post-war exodus from Italy carried many budding caterers to the West End and they quickly began to convert long-established cafés and snack

bars into stylish expresso bars. Others added to the growing numbers of
Italian restaurants in the area. Bar Italia on Frith Street was unveiled in
1949 and *La Terrazza* on Romily Street opened in 1959. There were other
Italian-owned businesses too. Lina Stores, an Italian delicatessen, opened on
Brewer Street in 1949, Angelucci's Coffee Stores at 23B Frith Street were
serving customers by 1955 and Old Compton Street's Camisa & Son,
another delicatessen, opened in 1961.

There was a fondly-remembered coffee bar at 93 Dean Street, a building
recorded by Crossrail before its demolition to make way for Crossrail's
new Tottenham Court Road Station. The building probably dated to the
mid-1800s and had a Victorian shopfront (Fig 83).[17] By 1900 Benjamin
Mark, a tailor, was operating from the building; he was replaced by 1915
by a confectioner called Andrea Cicconi. By 1950 Jack Carruthers was
running a café from the premises.[18] Although details are sketchy and rather
contradictory, Carruthers's café may have been transformed into a coffee
bar towards the end of the 1950s by an Italian named Gigi.[19] In the 1960s
it was known as *Les Enfants Terribles*, and became a favoured haunt for
London's beatniks.[20] It was still a café bar (*The Black Gardenia*) when it
closed in 2010.

The new coffee bars and restaurants of Soho found a ready market. No-one
alive could remember when the area had been respectable, and it had
gained the reputation as the habitue of intellectuals, writers and artists. Post-
war Soho (and parts of neighbouring Fitzrovia) were bywords for a slightly
studied loucheness much celebrated in later popular culture (Fig 84). It was

**Fig 83** (left) No. 93 Dean Street in the 1920s (LMA ref: SC/PHL/01//BOX 463); (right) By the 1950s it was a coffee bar and was still in use as a little bar when it closed in 2010

**Fig 84** The Soho Fair, Soho Square, 1956 (© Getty Images No 2643480/ Evening Standard 20 July 1957)

an atmosphere which drew in bedfellows from the performing arts, and from this cocktail emerged an entertainment industry that would spearhead the golden ages of British film in the 1940s and music in the 1960s.

## Music and media

Several of these strands coalesced in 1957 when Emeric Pressburger's film *Miracle in Soho* was released. Belinda Lee played Julia Gozzi, the daughter

There is an island in the great city of London — a little foreign island called Soho. Many nationalities live there whose everyday lives are composed of countless threads, of custom, of family. The Gozzi family live there, too, in a quiet little street; and, in particular Julia Gozzi and Michael Morgan for whom the threads snap . . . and the miracle happens. They never know the truth of it— only one man knows that; he saw it happen . . .

THE RANK ORGANISATION PRESENTS

**Miracle in SOHO**

starring

**JOHN GREGSON**
**BELINDA LEE**
**CYRIL CUSACK**

IN EASTMAN COLOUR

Written and Produced by
**EMERIC PRESSBURGER**
Directed by **JULIAN AMYES**

N.W. LONDON AUGUST 4th
N.E. LONDON AUGUST 11th
SOUTH LONDON AUGUST 18th
PRINCIPAL CITIES from AUGUST 4th

**Fig 85** Poster for
*Miracle in Soho*, 1957
(Rank Organisation)

of Italian immigrants living in Soho (Fig 85). The film was made by the Rank Organisation, which had its headquarters in nearby South Street in Mayfair. Rank's founder is generally credited with saving the British film industry. Soho Square, where three grout shafts were constructed as part of the preparatory work for Crossrail tunnelling beneath the 17th-century park, is still the home of the British Board of Film Classification and of 20th Century Fox.

Soho and neighbouring Fitzrovia remain the home of Britain's media and creative industries. This is best illustrated by two institutions on opposing corners of the district. The BBC, based in Broadcasting House behind Oxford Circus, does much to keep the post-production houses of the area busy. The north-eastern corner is marked by Denmark Street, which lies in the shadow of Centre Point and Crossrail's redevelopment of Tottenham Court Road Station. To this day the street is regarded as Britain's 'Tin Pan Alley'. The first music publisher, Lawrence Wright set up here in 1911 and he was soon followed by others. Wright was later to establish the *Melody Maker* in premises at No. 19. This influential music newspaper was joined on the newsstands in 1952 by the *New Musical Express*, founded at No. 5 Denmark Street.

The *100 Club* lies midway between the BBC and Denmark Street, in premises facing Tottenham Court Road Station's new western ticket hall. The home of British jazz since 1942, this little basement club had by the 1960s begun to attract British bands who were to form the 'British Invasion'. Although the rise of bands who wanted to compose their own

**Fig 86** *La Gioconda* Café in Denmark Street, Soho (© LMA)

music proved to be the death-knell of Denmark Street's music publishing trade, the street's recording studios and rehearsal rooms were soon attracting many of the biggest names in British rock music.[21] The street, and in particular *La Gioconda* café at No. 9, became a mecca for many of the household names of the 1960s (Fig 86).[22]

The industry was increasingly moribund as the 1970s wore on, but Soho was once again to be the scene of a cultural revolution when, in 1975, the Sex Pistols played in public for the first time at St Martins School of Art, a college located only a few dozen metres south of the Crossrail's new station at Tottenham Court Road. The band, whose members lived and rehearsed at 6 Denmark Street, almost single-handedly helped to usher in a new wave of musicians and designers, many of whom lived and worked in the area (Fig 87).[23]

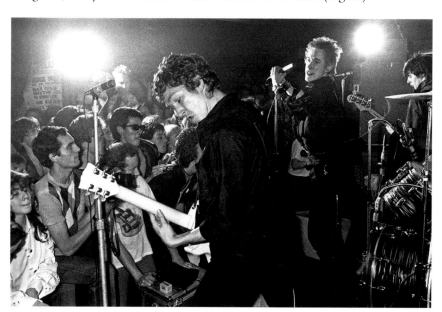

**Fig 87** The Sex Pistols at the 100 Club, 1976 (Hulton-Deutsch Collection/ CORBIS Image ID: HU002004)

### Clothing industry

Like the movement that grew around the Sex Pistols, the British Invasion was about more than simply music. For a short while after John Stephen had opened His Clothes, arguably the world's first male boutique, on Carnaby Street in 1958, clothing found itself perfectly aligned with Soho's musical revolution. Like Riservato before him, Stephen had identified a new market and before long he ran more than a dozen retail outlets on Carnaby Street alone.[24] Stephen's genius lay in understanding that a male population starting to embrace the consumerism and counter-culture of post-war Britain would welcome fashionable clothes. Until this moment, clothing had been manufactured by many small concerns catering for traditional and often very local markets. Soho was a centre for clothing and footwear manufacture and there were many such workshops. *Kelly's Post Office Directory for 1950*, for example, records that 97 to 99 Dean Street, a 1930s building demolished to make way for Crossrail's Tottenham Court Road Station, was the home of two gown manufacturers, a manufacturing furriers, Kosie Knitwear Ltd and Handmade Garments Ltd, manufacturers of 'smallwear' (Fig 88).

How had Soho become a centre for clothing manufacture? Part of the answer is the Huguenots, late 17th-century exiles from France who started to arrive in London just as the estates of Soho were beginning to be laid out. The relevant Survey of London volume estimates that the population of St Anne in 1711 included 3,450 French who formed two-fifths of the total for the parish.[25] (The parish of St Anne Soho was formed from part of the parish of St. Martin in the Fields in 1686). Most were lodgers, and amongst their number were skilled embroiderers and silk weavers. The bespoke nature of the products being made and the displaced status of those producing them were, and arguably still are, two of Soho's defining characteristics.

**Fig 88** The doorway of No 99 Dean Street shortly before the demolition

Any pretensions to grandeur that the inhabitants of Soho may have had were short-lived. By the second half of the 18th century Soho's wealthiest residents were departing for fashionable new areas to the west. Estates were dispersed and grand homes were sub-divided or demolished and replaced with multiple properties. The plushest parts of the area still housed wealthy aristocrats, but elsewhere a social decline was underway. One of the events that cemented Soho's character may have been the building of Regent Street by John Nash in 1816–1824 (Fig 89). This served, intentionally, to separate affluent Mayfair from the increasingly run-down streets of its neighbour.[26] During the first half of the 19th century Soho's population grew and by 1851 there were 327 inhabitants per acre - one of the highest figures in the whole of London. This was to be a high watermark. The middle classes, alarmed by increasing outbreaks of disease, began to drift away, leaving Soho to a declining number of poorer inhabitants.[27]

As the average income of Soho's population shrank it became ever more dependent on the production of clothing and footwear, especially after large numbers of Polish and Russian Jews arrived in the 1890s. By 1897 over 30% of the heads of households in the Soho, St Giles and Strand areas were employed in these industries, mostly in the piecework production of items for the bespoke tailors and couturiers on the other side of Regent

**Fig 89** *The Quadrant, Regent Street*, by Edmund Walker (© LMA)

Street.[28] Although women's involvement in the industry went largely unrecorded, Arthur Sherwell was to note that

> *'...by far the majority of the women workers in Soho are employed in the dress trades of the West. Of these a few are shirt and collar makers; a larger proportion dressmakers, mantlemakers, and milliners; while the great majority are tailoresses.'*[29]

Workers with the same skills tended to cluster together. This is illustrated by the contemporary street directories. In 1841, for example, Dean Street had nine tailors or clothiers, four milliners, four boot and shoemakers, three curriers or leatherworkers and a dressmaker. They made up 18% of the trades listed. In nearby Brewer Street 13% of the trades were in the industry (two tailor/clothiers, one boot/shoemaker, three woollen drapers and a silk mercer) whilst Regent Street boasted 128 clothing or footwear concerns, or 37% of the total. Amongst these were 37 milliners, nine furriers and seven silk mercers.

By 1895 the number of Dean Street properties involved in the clothing industry had declined to six, but there had been an increase in clothing-related activity in Brewer Street. There were fewer milliners in Regent Street, but more dressmakers. Of course, these numbers do not help in any attempt to estimate how many workers in total were involved. For example, Henry Heath's Hats alone employed upwards of 70 people.[30] The company's factory on Hollen Street (Fig 90), a stone's throw from

**Fig 90** (left) Henry Heath's Hat Factory on Hollen Street, Soho dates from 1887; (right) Denny's Uniforms still trades from premises in Soho (©Dennys Brands)

Crossrail's western ticket hall for Tottenham Court Road Station, survives, as does it showroom on Oxford Street. But while the factories may have closed, the local industry is far from dead. There are still many tailors, especially on Berwick Street, and there are clothes buyers, textile merchants and support services scattered throughout Soho and Fitzrovia. Examples abound: Taylor's Buttons on Cleveland Street, for example, has been supplying hand-covered fabric buttons to the trade for over 100 years. Denny's Uniforms, which started making and retailing garments for the local restaurant and hotel trade in 1840, still has a shop on Dean Street, even if their manufacturing is now undertaken in China (Fig 90).

## Coachworks and carriage building

As London grew the necessity for transport increased, and in affluent areas a sizeable carriage industry emerged (Fig 91). In a class-conscious society, keeping a carriage was a mark of wealth, status and character. In *Sense and Sensibility* Jane Austen's frightful social climber, Lucy Steele, explains to Elinor Dashwood that *"[Mr. Richardson] makes a monstrous deal of money, and they keep their own coach."*[31] Indeed, Austen's characters are often to be found dashing about west London in their chaises, chariots and curricles.

A carriage industry emerged serving the expanding population of West London. By 1871 there were over 600 coachmen and grooms living on the Grosvenor Estate, an area loosely defined as Mayfair and Belgravia.[32] When this number is added to the 489 people on the estate who cited the independent transport trade as their occupation the size of the industry becomes clear.[33]

It was inevitable that London's coachbuilders would establish themselves
close to the wealthiest parts of the capital. John Hatchett, for example, a
master of the Coach Makers Company in 1785 and the most famous
coach-maker of his day, chose Long Acre in Covent Garden. The street
retained its dominance as a centre for coachbuilding well into the motor
age, as a map of the businesses on the street in 1916 shows.[34] Although a
number of motor manufacturers - Fiat Motors Ltd (at Nos 37–38),
General Motors (Nos 135–136), Daimler-Mercedes (at Nos 127–130)
and Morgan & Co Ltd – were now present, an equal number of coachbuilders remained.[35]

Alongside the well-known coachbuilders were smaller concerns, most of
which were involved in providing servicing and repairs for coaches. One
of these was John George Crowe, a coachbuilder who in the mid 19th
century operated from Cock Yard.[36] The yard lay at the north-eastern edge
of the Grosvenor Estate, beside the Davies Street block that Crossrail is
redeveloping as Bond Street Station's new western ticket hall. Studying the
history of the yard reveals the extent of the horse-drawn industry in
Georgian Mayfair. Cock Yard had developed from the stable yards of two
taverns, The Three Horseshoes and The One Tun, which at one time had
faced each other across the former valley of the diverted River Tyburn
(Fig 92). Crossrail's archaeological excavations of the Davies Street block
showed that reclamation of the river channel had begun during the mid
1700s, suggesting the yards would have been laid out once this reclamation
was complete.[37] The picture revealed by the results of the archaeological
excavation - of the dumping of household refuse by local inhabitants -

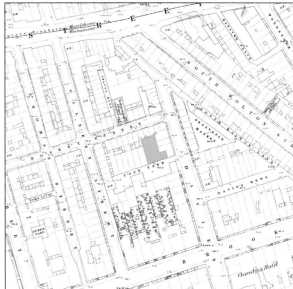

is brought to vivid life by the discovery of several horse carcasses in the river channel. It is not beyond the realms of possibility that these were the discarded remains of beasts which had not long since been stabled in the tavern yards.

During the 1820s new houses were erected on the Davies Street frontage. To the rear the builder Seth Smith added a large two-storey workshop and a line of coach houses and stables, all of which opened onto the newly formed Cock Yard (Fig 93). The south side of Cock Yard was formed by the coach houses and stables of houses fronting Brook Street.[38] In 1839 these are referred to twice in court records. Charles Davies, a coachman in the service of Eliza Parry of Brook Street, gave evidence in a theft trial that he had noticed lead missing from the roof of a stable in Cock Yard. In the other reference, Samuel Lofting stated that he was employed at Mr Mivart's stables in Cock Yard, which presumably lay behind Mivart's Brook Street hotel.[39]

By 1852 the yard was home to a carman (Thomas Turner), a farrier (William Sinnet) and a jobman (Charles Day). It is easy from these references to imagine a yard alive with the sound of iron-shod hooves on cobbles and the ring of the hammer on the anvil. These sounds may have carried on well into the night, as a passage by W J Gordon in 1893 reminds us.

> *The stabling in a London mews has not the best of reputations, and its accommodation compares unfavourably with that obtainable at a country town; in fact, it is owing in a great measure to the stable difficulty that so many people job their horses during the London season. The horse of pleasure is not like the horse of trade; he is worked at all hours, but rarely with*

**Fig 92** (left) Detail from Horwood's 1799 map of Mayfair, showing the stable yards of *The Three Horseshoes* and *The One Tun*
(© MOTCO)

**Fig 93** (right) The 1872-1873 1:1,056 Town Plan shows (in red) a large building in Cock Yard that may have been Seth Smith's workshop
(© Groundsure)

*regularity; he is kept healthy with exercise instead of work; and consequently
he has to be carefully looked after, and wants the best of housing, which in
London he does not always get.*[40]

**Fig 94** Remains of a workshop, possibly a forge or farriers, were uncovered during excavation for Bond Street station's new western ticket hall

During the excavation of the Davies Street block parts of Smith's 1820's workshop were uncovered. A number of walls survived, and a series of three parallel arched chambers beside a brick (later flagstone) floor were found (Fig 94). The chambers were packed with ash and ironworking waste, possibly evidence that the remains represented a forge or farriers.

As the motor car gained acceptance coach houses began to be adapted to accommodate them. At the same time, the number of motor manufacturers with a West End presence rose rapidly. Argyll established themselves at Newman Street, Albion built an office and garage in Poland Street, and Ariel settled at New Bond Street.[41] The supremacy of the motor vehicle was illustrated when Austin, also keen to establish a West End presence, took over the former Oxford Street showrooms of coachbuilders Holland & Holland.[42] Other coachbuilders more successfully managed the transition from horse power to the internal combustion engine. Hoopers & Co. (Coachbuilders) Ltd, for example, who had been founded on the Haymarket in 1805, ended their days making limousines in an Art Deco factory at Park Royal. Barker & Co. were another West End company that had started in 1710 by making luxury horse-drawn carriages. When Hoopers took them over in 1938 they built them a bespoke factory in Willesden, not far from their Park Royal works, and close to Crossrail's Old Oak Common depot.

By the time Hoopers collapsed in 1959 the era of the separate car chassis, and the companies who crafted bodies over them, was over. A new generation of coachbuilders instead turned their attention to a car which had been launched that year and was to become the car of the Swinging Sixties. The Mini had been an instant hit with the newly-enriched fashion designers and musicians of the West End, and Bill Wood and Les Pickett, former Hooper employees, saw their opportunity. Wood and Pickett's Park Royal workshops were soon turning out bespoke Minis for celebrities like the model Twiggy (Fig 95 left). An even more famous adaptation of the same model was offered by Harold Radford (Coachbuilders) Limited, again of Park Royal (Fig 95 right).

Wood and Pickett, and Radford were the modern-day equivalents of Soho's 17th-century embroiderers and silk weavers. Like the Huguenot craftsmen who had settled beside the Royal Court to supply wealthy

tastes, the bespoke coachbuilders of Park Royal sold to the new royalty of post-war London. And whilst the coachbuilders may have in turn fallen by the wayside, the connectivity that Crossrail promises will ensure that west London continues to produce the newly wealthy and new industries to serve them.

**Fig 95** (left) Sixties model Twiggy behind the wheel of a Wood and Pickett Mini; (right) John Lennon in a Radford Mini de Ville (both © Getty Images)

## Biographical portraits

### ELIZABETH GARRETT ANDERSON (1836-1917)

Elizabeth Garrett was born in Whitechapel in 1836 and lived there until the family moved briefly to West London and then to Aldeburgh in Suffolk in 1841. Elizabeth grew up in a family that encouraged her education and when she was 13 her father paid for her to study at the Boarding School for Ladies in Blackheath. She had an interest in joining the medical profession and so in 1860 she started work as a surgery nurse at Middlesex Hospital. At the same time as working as a nurse she also studied medicine both privately and at the Middlesex.

In the 1860s she became the first woman to become a doctor in Britain, but to qualify she had to study in Paris. She found it impossible to find employment as a doctor in a hospital and so in 1865 she opened her own medical practice at 20 Upper Berkeley Street, London. In 1866 she also set up St Mary's Dispensary for Women and Children at 69 Seymour Place, Bryanston Square, Marylebone using philanthropic donations. This dispensary and later hospital allowed women and children to be treated by female medical staff. The hospital also provided aspiring female doctors with clinical teaching so they could qualify at the London School of Medicine for Women.

Elizabeth fought against negativity towards female doctors and her efforts were rewarded in 1876 with a change in the law, which allowed women to practice medicine. Throughout her life she also campaigned for the rights of women and wrote many articles, some of which were published in the national newspapers. In December 1896 Elizabeth wrote a letter to The Times about the struggle for women to become doctors:

> *Step by Step and with much effort, progress had been made till, at the present time, nearby all the medical examining bodies in this country admit women to their examinations and diplomas on the same terms as men and several medical schools exist in which they can be educated either separately or side by side with men.*
> (*The Times*, Friday 11th December, 1896)

**Fig 96** Elizabeth Garrett Anderson (Wellcome Library, London. Copyrighted work available under Creative Commons Attribution only licence CC BY 4.0, Image No. V0025970)

In 1871 she married James George Skelton Anderson and together they had three children: Louisa, Margaret and Alan. Louisa also became a doctor and a militant suffragette before serving in France during the First World War.[43]

### BEATRICE LIZZIE WAKEMAN (NÉE WELCH) (1882-1931)

Beatrice Lizzie Welch was born in Chertsey in 1882 and in her teens moved to London to look for work. She kept a diary from December 1899 to May 1900 and this allows a glimpse of six months of her working life as a drapers clerk for Robinson and Cleaver's at 170 Regent Street. Whilst working in London she lived for a while in accommodation that was likely to have been provided for by her employer which she shared with her female colleagues. Beatrice appeared to enjoy sharing a dormitory where she read ghost stories to her friends; they got into pillow fights and danced on the beds. This type of employer's accommodation was called the 'living in system' and food and lodging were provided by keeping wages low. Male and female staff that 'lived in' had to abide by strict rules and if they broke them they were under threat of losing both their job and somewhere to live.

A WORK ROOM.

**Fig 97** London Drapers workroom (after Belloc Lowndes 1901, p 209)

In her diary Beatrice mentions several of the male managers and how she tries to avoid getting caught by them. Mr Pritchard appears to have been one of the managers of the upstairs drapery section where Beatrice worked. When he was away the girls had more fun *'When the cat is away the mice will play'*. She also liked to sneak down to talk to her friend Debs who was an assistant in the gentlemen's shop downstairs. However, to do so she needed to avoid the managers Mr Hanbury and Mr Lack. On February 28th 1900 she writes *'went down to talk to Deb and Mr Hanbury always catches me there'*.[44]

Beatrice is likely to have worked a 45-60 hour week at Robinson and Cleaver's and her diary suggests that on a busy day on the 12th March 1900 *'we don't close now until half past six'*. She also had to work until early afternoon on a Saturday and so Sunday was her only day off. The hours Beatrice worked in 1900 were less than the average shop workers of just five years previously. Evidence given in Parliament for the Shops Early Closing Bill of 1895 suggested that the average hours of work London shop assistants were between 68 and 100 per week.

By the census of 1901 she had moved out of live-in accommodation and was staying with her sister Lilian and her sister's husband Sidney Metcalf in North Wimbledon. It is likely she kept her job at Robinson and Cleaver's as the Census of March 1901 describes her as a 'drapers clerk'. One of the reasons she may have wanted to move out of 'living in' accommodation was to gain more freedom and escape the rule of celibacy. By 1903 Beatrice had met Harry William Wakeman who she married two years later in 1905 in Wandsworth. A later note in the diary from 29th August 1910 recorded how she had been married for over five years and had two young sons. Beatrice Wakeman lived to the age of 49 and died in Islington in 1931.

## NOTES

1    Noon 2008, 54-55, 59
2    Brent Council 2004, 12
3    Wallop 2012
4    2011 Census First Results: London Boroughs' Population by Age and Sex, GLA Intelligence, Census Information Scheme
5    The information in this paragraph is drawn largely from Atkins 2013, 44. The history and development of Crosse & Blackwell in Soho is also detailed in Jeffries *et al.* 2016. The piccalilli label illustrated was the cause of a legal dispute between Crosse & Blackwell (plaintiffs) and Crabbe & Company (defendants) that took place in 1867. The label was reproduced with the report of the proceedings in Robertson 1914, 565-567. The Reform Club is a Gentleman's club in Pall Mall historically associated with the Liberal Party, but perhaps as famous for the being the start and end location in Jules Verne's 'Around the World in Eighty Days'.

6   'Soho Square Area: Portland Estate, No. 20 Soho Square', pp 69-72 in Sheppard 1966

7   Atkins 2013, 45

8   Mayhew 1865, 174-88

9   Atkins 2013, 46

10  'Shaftesbury Avenue and Charing Cross Road', pp 296-312 in Sheppard 1966

11  The full results of the archaeological work on this site are provided in Jeffries *et al.* 2016

12  Atkins 2013, 41, 43

13  Sherwell 1897, 61

14  Walkowitz 2011, 419-30

15  Partington 2009; Partington 2013

16  Ellis 2004, 225-45

17  Recorded by Wessex Archaeology before demolition: Wessex Archaeology April 2010, *Crossrail Tottenham Court Station, Soho, London: Non-Listed Built Heritage Recording* (reference 72213.0,) (C134-XRL-T1-RGN-CRG03-5001)

18  Kelly's *Post-Office Directories*

19  Pip Granger records that it was Betty Passes who was running the café in 1957 (Granger 2009, 307); www.lesenfantsterrible.adrianstern.com suggests that Lucio Davanzo purchased the lease on the premises in 1961 (accessed 14 July 14)

20  Granger 2009, 289

21  In 1964 the Rolling Stones recorded their first album at Regent Sound Studios, then as now based at No. 4 Denmark Street.

22  Humphreys 2003, 119

23  Graves-Brown and Schofield 2011, 1385–1401

24  Horwell 2004

25  'General Introduction', pp 1-19 in Sheppard 1966

26  Ehrman 2008, 174-175

27  Soho's population fell by 31.9% between 1861 and 1891 (Sherwell 1897, Part I, Chapter I); Charles Booth (1891, 27) categorised 42.4% of population of Soho as poor in the 1890s. By contrast only 2.7% of the population of Mayfair classified as in poverty. Booth gave an overall figure of 21% in poverty for West London, which included both Mayfair and Soho.

28  Sherwell 1897, 61

29  Sherwell 1897, Chapter VII Dressmaking

30  *Post Office London Directory, 1841 (Part 1: Street, Commercial, & Trades) and Post Office London Directory, 1895 (Part 4: Trades & Professional)*; http://virtualvictorian.blogspot.co.uk/2010/07/henry-heaths-top-hats-extravagant.html accessed 21 Jul 14

31  Austen 1811, chapter 38, p.268

32  'The Social Character of the Estate: The Censuses of 1841 and 1871', pp. 93-98 in Sheppard 1977.

33  Loc. cit.

34  Morrison and Minnis, 2012, 51

35  *Post Office London Directory, 1914. (Part 4: Trades & Professional Directory)*; Vickers 1994, 1

36  *Post Office directory* 1852

37  Oxford Archaeology/Ramboll, 2012, *C254 Archaeology West Archaeological Excavation at Bond Street Station: Interim Report* (C254-OXF-W-RGN-C125-50002 Rev 2.0)

38  'Davies Street Area: St. Anslem's Place', pp. 82-83 in Sheppard 1980

39  *Old Bailey Proceedings Online* (www.oldbaileyonline.org, version 7.2, 28 April 2016), February 1839, trial of JOHN BROAD JOHN HOLTON (t18390204-781)

40  Gordon 1893, 105

41  Morrison and Minnis 2012, 51-52

42  Ibid, 52

43  Elston 2005; London Remembers, 2014, Plaque: Elizabeth Garrett Anderson - W1, URL:http://www.londonremembers.com/memorials/elizabeth-garrett-anderson-w1 Date Accessed: 21 July 2014

44   Eccleston, Mark, 2009, Diary of Beatrice Welch 1899-1910, main entries 23
     December 1899 until May 1900, MS187, Cadbury Research Library: Special
     Collections, University of Birmingham URL: http://calmview.bham.ac.uk/Record.
     aspx?src=CalmView.Catalog&id=XMS187%2f1&pos=3 Date accessed: 21 July 2014.
     Special permission received by Helen Fisher, Archivist Cadbury Research Library:
     Special Collections on 22 July 2014 to use the information from the database entry
     and a short quote from the diary.

# BIBLIOGRAPHY

Andrews, D & Merriman, N, 1986 'A prehistoric timber structure at Richmond Terrace, Whitehall', *Trans London Middlesex Archaeol Soc* **37**, 17–21

Atkins, P, 2013 'Vinegar and Sugar: the Early History of Factory-made Jams, Pickles and Sauces in Britain', 41-55, in Oddy, D J and Drouard, A, (eds), *The Food Industries of Europe in the Nineteenth and Twentieth Centuries*, Ashgate

Austen, Jane, 1811 *Sense and Sensibility*, Penguin edition

Baker, T F T, Bolton, D K and Croot, P E C, 1989 *A History of the County of Middlesex: Volume 9, Hampstead, Paddington*, ed. C R Elrington, London *British History Online* http://www.british-history.ac.uk/vch/middx/vol9 [accessed 21 March 2016].

Barker, F, and Jackson, P, 1990 *The History of London in Maps*, Guild Publishing, London

Barton, N J, 1962 *The Lost Rivers of London,* Phoenix House, 1962

Bates, M R. Champness, C, Haggart, A, Macphail, Parfitt, S A, Schwenninger, J-L, 2014 Early Devensian sediments and palaeovenvironmental evidence from the excavations at the Royal Oak Portal Paddington, West London, UK, *Proc. Geol. Assoc.* 125, Issue 1, 41–55 (doi:10.1016/j.pgeola.2013.06.001)

Belloc-Lowndes, Mrs 1901 'London's Drapers' pp 209-15 in Sims, G R (ed) *Living London: Its Work and Its Play, Its Humour and Its Pathos, Its Sights and Its Scenes, Vol 2, section 2*, Cassell & Co, London

Booth, C (ed) 1891 *Labour and Life of the People. Vol II*, Williams and Norgate, London and Edinburgh

Boulnois, H, 1895 *The construction of carriageways & footways*, Biggs & Co, London, 61

Bramah, E, 1972 *Tea and coffee: a modern view of three hundred years of tradition*, Hutchinson

Brent Council, 2004 *London Borough of Brent Unitary Development Plan 2004*

Bridgeland, D R, 2006 'The Middle and Upper Pleistocene sequence in the Lower Thames; a record of Milankovitch climatic fluctuation and early human occupation of southern Britain. Henry Stopes Memorial Lecture'. *Proceedings of the Geologists Association* **117**, 281-305

Brooke, C.N.L, 1975 *London 800-1216, The shaping of a city*, University of California Press, Berkley and Los Angeles

Carey, B, 2003 'The extraordinary Negro', Ignatius Sancho, Joseph Jekyll, and the problem of biography' *British Journal for Eighteenth Century Studies* **26**, 1-14

City of Westminster 2008 *Conservation Area Audit 10. Harley Street*. http://www3. westminster.gov.uk/docstores/publications_store/Harley Street CAA SPD.pdf [accessed 14 April 2016]

Clout, H D (ed), 1991 *The Times London History Atlas*, Times Books/Harper Collins, London

Clow, D, 2008 'From Macadam to Asphalt: The Paving of the Streets of London in the Victorian Era. Part 2: Wood, Asphalt and Other Surfaces', *London's Industrial Archaeology* No. **9**, 2008, 3-14

Cockburn, J S, King H P F, and McDonnell, K G T (eds) 1969 *A History of the County of Middlesex: Volume 1, Physique, Archaeology, Domesday, Ecclesiastical Organization, the Jews, Religious Houses, Education of Working Classes to 1870, Private Education from Sixteenth Century*, (London, 1969), British History Online http://www.british-history.ac.uk/vch/middx/vol1 [accessed 18 March 2016]

Compass Archaeology 2011, 26 North Road Highgate, London Borough of Haringey Archaeological Post Excavation Assessment, unpublished Client Report November 2011

Cowie, R, and Blackmore, L, with Davis, A, Keily, J, and Rielly, K, 2012 *Lundenwic: excavations in Middle Saxon London, 1987–2000*, MOLA Monograph series 63

Dow, A, 2014 *The Railway: British track since 1804*, Barnsley

Ehrman, E, 2008 'Regency Shopping', 174-175, in Ross, C & Clark, J (eds), *London: the Illustrated History*, Museum of London,

Ellis, M, 2004 *The Coffee House: A Cultural History*, Weidenfeld & Nicholson

Elston, M.A, 2005, 'Anderson, Elizabeth Garrett (1836–1917)', Oxford Dictionary of National Biography, Oxford University Press, 2004; online edn, URL: http://www.oxforddnb.com/view/article/30406,Date accessed 21 July 2014

Fowler, L, and Taylor, R, 2013 *At the limits of Lundenwic: excavations in the north-west of Middle Saxon London at St Martin's Courtyard*, MOLA Archaeology Studies Series 27

Gater, G H, and Hiorns, F R (eds) 1940 *Survey of London: Volume 20, St Martin-in-The-Fields, Pt III: Trafalgar Square and Neighbourhood*, (London, 190), *British History Online* http://www.british-history.ac.uk/survey-london/vol20/pt3 [accessed 9 March 2016]

Gillings, A, 2006 *Brunel*, Haus Publishing, London

Gordon, W J, 1893 *The Horse-World of London*, The Religious Tracts Society, London

Granger, P, 2009 *Up West*, Corgi

Graves-Brown, P and Schofield, J, 2011 'The Filth and the Fury: 6 Denmark Street (London) and the Sex Pistols', *Antiquity* **85**, 1385–1401

Hey, G, with Robinson, M, 2011 Chapter 10 –Mesolithic communities in the Thames Valley: living in the natural environment, 193-220, in Morigia, A, Shreve, M, Whire, M, Hey, G, Garwood, P, Robinson, M, Barclay, A and Bradley, P, *Thames Through Time. The archaeology of the gravel terraces of the Upper and Middle Thames. Early prehistory to 1500 BC*, Thames Valley Landscapes Monograph No. 32, Oxford Archaeology

Horwell, V, 2004 Obituary of John Stephen, *The Guardian*, published 8 Feb 2004

Humphreys, R, 2003 *The Rough Guide to London*, Rough Guides

Jeffries, N, with Blackmore, L, and Sorapure, D, 2016 *Crosse and Blackwell 1830-1920: A British Food Manufacturer in London's West End*, Crossrail Archaeology Series 6

Keene, D, 2004 'William fitz Osbert (d. 1196)', *Oxford Dictionary of National Biography*, Oxford University Press, 2004 [http://www.oxforddnb.com/view/article/9621, accessed 10 July 2014]

Kent, J, 1978 The London area in the Late Iron Age: an interpretation of the earliest coins, 53–8, in Bird, J, Chapman, H, and Clark, J (eds), *Collectanea Londoniensia: studies in London archaeology and history presented to Ralph Merrifield*, London & Middlesex Archaeol Soc Special Paper 2, London

Lewis, J S C, with Rackham, J, 2011 *Three Ways Wharf, Uxbridge: a Late glacial and Early Holocene hunter-gatherer site in the Colne Valley*, MOLA Monograph Series 51

Malcolm, G, Bowsher, D, and Cowie, R, 2003 *Middle Saxon London: excavations at the Royal Opera House 1989–99*, MOLA Monograph series 15, London

Mason, E (ed) 1988 *Westminster Abbey Charters, 1066 – c.1214 London Record Society 25*, (London, 1988), *British History Online* http://www.british-history.ac.uk/london-record-soc/vol25 [accessed 23 July 2014]

Mason, E, 1996 *Westminster Abbey and Its People C.1050-c.1216*, Studies in the History of Medieval Religion 9, Boydell Press, Suffolk

Matthews, E C, 1917 'The development of Paddington station, VI', *GWR Magazine* September 1917, 175-77

Mayhew, H, 1865 'The establishment of Messrs Crosse and Blackwell, sauce and pickle manufacturers', 174-88, in Idem (ed.), *The shops and companies of London, Volume 1*, Strand Printing and Publishing Co. Ltd,

Morrison, K A and Minnis, J, 2012 *Carscapes*, Yale University Press

MOLA, 2012 Bond Street Station Upgrade LUL Works London W1, Archaeological Watching Brief and Standing Building Recording Progress Report, 2 Stratford Place

MOLA, 2014 Basement Vault of the Oriental Club Stratford House, Stratford Place London WC1 City of Westminister

MOLA, 1996 Curzon Gate, Park Lane, London W1. An Archaeological Evaluation, unpublished client report,

MOLA, 2000 *The archaeology of Greater London. An assessment of archaeological evidence for human presence in the area now covered by Greater London*, Museum of London

Noon, G, 2008 *Noon, with a View*, Whittles Publishing

Page, W (ed) 1909 *A History of the County of London: Volume 1, London Within the Bars, Westminster and Southwark*, (London), *British History Online* http://www.british-history.ac.uk/vch/london/vol1 [accessed 19 March 2016]

Partington, M, 2009 'The London Coffee Bar of the 1950s – teenage occupation of an amateur space?' in *Occupation: Negotiations with Constructed Space (Interior Architecture Conference)*, University of Brighton, Grand Parade, Brighton, July 2-4 2009 http://eprints.uwe.ac.uk/10843

Partington, M, 2013 'Espresso, Exoticism and Earthenware: The London Coffee Bar Ceramics of the Picassoettes (William Newland, Margaret Hine and Nicholas Vergette) 1952-1966', 90-99, in Dahn, J and Jones, J (eds) *Interpreting Ceramics, Selected Essays*, Bath: Wunderkammer Press

PCA 2002 Report of an evaluation and watching brief at the proposed site of the Diana, Princess of Wales Memorial Fountain, West Carriage Road, Hyde Park, Westminster, unpublished client report October 2002

PCA 2003 Assessment of an Archaeological Evaluation and Excavation on the site of The Diana, Princess of Wales, Memorial Fountain, Hyde Park, Westminster, October 2003

Ponsford, M, and Jackson, R, 1997 Post-medieval Britain and Ireland in 1996, *Post-Medieval Archaeology* **31**, 257-332

Porter, R, 1994 *London, A Social History*, Hamish Hamilton, London

Robertson, M, 1914 *English Reports Annotated, 1866-1900*, Volume 1, The Reports & Digest Syndicate Ltd

Ross, C, and Clark, R. (eds.) 2008 *London the Illustrated History*, Museum of London, Penguin Books, London

Shelley, A, with Brown, R, 2016 *From Brunel to British Rail. The Railway Heritage of the Crossrail Route*, Crossrail Archaeology Series No.4

Sheppard, F H W (ed) 1960 *Survey of London: Volumes 29 and 30, St James Westminster, Part 1*, (London), *British History Online* http://www.british-history.ac.uk/survey-london/vols29-30/pt1 [accessed 18 March 2016].

Sheppard, F H W (ed) 1966 *Survey of London: Volumes 33 and 34, St Anne Soho*, (London), *British History Online* http://www.british-history.ac.uk/survey-london/vols33-4 [accessed 10 July 2014]

Sheppard, F H W (ed) 1970 *Survey of London: Volume 36, Covent Garden*, (London), *British History Online* http://www.british-history.ac.uk/survey-london/vol36 [accessed 19 March 2016]

Sheppard, F H W (ed) 1977 *Survey of London: Volume 39, the Grosvenor Estate in Mayfair, Part 1 (General History)*, Sheppard (London), *British History Online* http://www.british-history.ac.uk/survey-london/vol39/pt1 [accessed 12 April 2016].

Sheppard, F H W (ed) 1980 *Survey of London: Volume 40, the Grosvenor Estate in Mayfair, Part 2 (The Buildings)* (London), *British History Online* http://www.british-history.ac.uk/survey-london/vol40/pt2 [accessed 29 March 2016].

Sherwell, A, 1897 *Life in West London: A Study and a Contrast,* Methuen

Summerson, J, 1945 *Georgian London*, Pleiades Books, London

Temple, P (ed) *Survey of London: Volume 47, Northern Clerkenwell and Pentonville*, (London. *British History Online* http://www.british-history.ac.uk/survey-london/vol47 [accessed 12 April 2016]

Turvey, R, 1996 'Street Mud, Dust and Noise', *The London Journal* vol. **21**, no. 2, 131-48

Vickers, R, 1994 'Coachbuilding in London', *London's Industrial Archaeology* No.**5**, GLIAS

Walford, E, 1878, *Old and New London. Volume 3*, London, Cassell & Co

Walkowitz, J R, 2011 'The Emergence of Cosmopolitan Soho', 419-430, in Bridge, G and Watson, S (eds), 2012, *The New Blackwell Companion to the City*, Wiley-Blackwell

Wallop, H, 2012 'London's 'bread basket' wrestles to keep costs down as even foodies cut back', *Daily Telegraph*, published 18 Feb 2012 http://www.telegraph.co.uk/finance/newsbysector/retailandconsumer/9090329/Londons-bread-basket-wrestles-to-keep-costs-down-as-even-foodies-cut-back.html

Waterhouse, P, 2004, 'Wyatt, Sir Matthew Digby (1820–1877)', rev. John Martin Robinson, *Oxford Dictionary of National Biography*, Oxford University Press, http://www.oxforddnb.com/view/article/30109, Date accessed 14 Aug 2014

Weinreb, B, and Hibbert, C, 2008 *The London Encyclopedia*, Macmillan

## Crossrail reports

Crossrail 2008, *Tottenham Court Road Station Site Specific Archaeological Detailed Desk-Based Assessment* (CR-SD-TCR-EN-SR-00001)

Oxford Archaeology/Gifford 2011, *Archaeology West – Contract No. C254 Archaeological Watching Briefs in the vicinity of Bond Street Stations Event Code XSC10. Interim Statement.* (C254_OXF-A-RGN-C125-50001)

Oxford Archaeology/Ramboll 2012, *C254 Archaeology West Archaeological Excavation at Bond Street Station: Interim Report* (C254-OXF-W-RGN-C125-50002 Rev 2.0)

Oxford Archaeology/Ramboll 2015a, *C254 Archaeology West Archaeological Works at Paddington_ XSD10 Eastbourne Terrace Wooden Sett Roadway Characterisation* (C254-OXF-T1-RGN-CRG03-50109 rev3)

Oxford Archaeology/Ramboll 2015b, *Building Recording, Departures Road, Paddington Station* (C254-OXF-T1-RGN-CRG03-50214)

Oxford Archaeology/Ramboll 2015c, *Building Recording: Paddington Station Milk Ramp* (C254-OXF-T1-RGN-CRG03-50215 Rev 2)

Wessex Archaeology April 2010, *Crossrail Tottenham Court Station, Soho, London: Non-Listed Built Heritage Recording* (reference 72213.0) (C134-XRL-T1-RGN-CRG03-5001)

## On-line resources

*British History Online* http://www.british-history.ac.uk

Brycchan Carey http://www.brycchancarey.com

Cadbury Research Library: Special Collections, University of Birmingham
    http://calmview.bham.ac.uk

*Dictionary of Art Historians* http://www.dictionaryofarthistorians.org

*Les Enfants Terribles* - www.lesenfantsterrible.adrianstern.com

*London Remembers* - http://www.londonremembers.com/

*Old Bailey Proceedings online* http://www.oldbaileyonline.org

*Oxford Dictionary of National Biography* http://www.oxforddnb.com

*Victorianweb*, http://www.victorianweb.org

*The Virtual Victorian* http://virtualvictorian.blogspot.co.uk

*Wild Peak blog* http://thewildpeak.wordpress.com

*100 Great Black Britons* http://www.100greatblackbritons.com

http://www.rail.co.uk

http://www.railway-technology.com

*Masterpieces of Ballet Design*

PETER WILLIAMS

# Masterpieces of Ballet Design

PHAIDON PRESS

Phaidon Press Limited
Littlegate House, St Ebbe's Street, Oxford

First published 1981
© 1981 Phaidon Press Limited
All rights reserved

ISBN 0 7148 2042 3
Library of Congress Catalog Card Number: 79-56804

Produced by Graphic Consultants International Pte Ltd
Printed in Singapore

*Frontispiece:* ROUBEN TER-ARUTUNIAN: *Pierrot lunaire*
(Bruce in title role, Ballet Rambert prod.); first given at a
recital in New York, 1962; by Ballet Rambert at the
Richmond Theatre, London, 1967.
(Photo: Anthony Crickmay)

*Cover:* NICHOLAS GEORGIADIS: *House of Birds*
(costume). See Plate 67.

# Contents

# Acknowledgements

*The author and publishers would like to thank the following for their help in compiling this book:*
Annette Armstrong, Sir Frederick Ashton, Nadine Baylis, Sir Cecil Beaton, Elaine Bromwich, Peter Farmer, Sir Robert Helpmann, Jean Hugo, John Piper and Peter Wilson.

ILLUSTRATIONS
Alwyn Nikolais Dance Co., New York: 77
Bibliothèque Nationale, Paris: 1
Bibliothèque-Musée de l'Opéra, Paris: 6, 2
Courtauld Institute of Art (by Courtesy of the Trustees of the Chatsworth Settlement): 3

Dansmuseet, Stockholm (Rolf de Mare Collection): 13, 16
Royal Ballet Benevolent Fund: 54
Theatre Museum, Victoria and Albert Museum: 4, 5, 7, 72
Wadsworth Atheneum, Hartford, Conn., The Ella Gallup Sumner and Mary Catlin Sumner Collection: 14, 18, 35, 43, 50
ADAGP: 41, 42, 43, 46, 47, 49, 53, 58, 63, 69, 71
SPADEM: 36, 37, 38, 39, 44, 45, 48, 50, 51, 52
*The publishers have endeavoured to credit all known persons holding copyright or reproduction rights for the illustrations in this book.*

Since the dawn of time there has been dance—in celebration of the changing seasons, birth, marriage, of victory in battle; in rituals of mourning, or in praise of some deity. Dance is an instinct inherent in man, since even a child will jump around and move its arms in expression of joy or excitement; instinctively it will bow down or throw itself to the ground in moments of sorrow. It stands to reason that this sense of movement will, in the adult, become more formalized in ceremonial and ritual.

Although we know that dance was an essential part of ancient Egyptian ritual and Greek drama, and that until the Middle Ages folk dances and more formal Court dances were generally practised throughout Europe (especially in the Mediterranean countries) it was not until the late fifteenth century that dance found a form that may be related to what we now think of as ballet (a word that originated as 'balleto' in Gugliemo Ebro's *Treatise on the Art of Dancing*, 1463).

Renaissance Italy was the birthplace of a theatrical dance form: the masque, an amalgam of song, dance and declamation. At Tortona in 1489 one Bergonzio di Botta devised a spectacle, virtually a form of cabaret, for a banquet celebrating the marriage of the Duke of Milan to Isabel of Aragon. Each course was introduced by dances appropriate to the nature of the dish being served—the fish, for instance, being brought on with dances about Neptune and the sea, the meat with dances about Diana and the chase, and so on. There does not appear to be any record of who designed this entertainment but it started a fashion that spread through the Courts of Europe.

The Italian influence spread to France when Catherine de' Medici became Queen. She was responsible for promoting similar and more elaborate entertainments, often with political implications, to honour various occasions. The most famous of these was *Ballet comique de la Reine* in 1581, devised by Balthasar de Beaujoyeux (formerly the Italian Baldassarino di Belgiojoso) to celebrate the wedding of the Duc de Joyeuse to the Queen's sister, Marguerite of Lorraine. The subject—hardly suitable for such an occasion, one would have thought—concerned a prisoner escaping the spell of Circe and seeking assistance from the king. Other prisoners (Circe's rejected suitors whom she has bewitched into animal shapes) are released by Mercury, Pan and other gods; she is finally struck down by a thunderbolt from Jupiter. The spectacle, which lasted over ten hours, ended with a 'Grand Ballet' during which the dancers moved around in geometric floor patterns. Apart from this interesting development of choreographic form, *Ballet comique de la Reine* is important in that it was designed by the Court painter, Jacques Patin. It was also an early example of ballet-in-the-round. The spectators were ranged in tiers along each side of the Great Hall of the Petit-Bourbon Palace, with the Royal party at one end and Circe's palace and garden at the opposite end. On the right side of the hall was a small structure representing the Grove of Pan, on the left a cloud structure to house the deities. Patin's dresses were apparently very splendid, made in rich fabrics heavily embroidered and encrusted with precious stones.

But although *Ballet comique de la Reine* was a landmark in the development of ballet as an art form, from the design aspect the main interest lay in the elaborate and often most imaginative dresses. In Italy, however, during the mid-sixteenth century, there was a great revival of interest in ancient Greek and Roman art, including architecture and the art of perspective. Sebastiano Serlio, inspired by the works of Vitruvius, created architectural settings which reflected the nature of the masque, whether heroic tragedy or rustic comedy. With the stage flanked by heavily-constructed architectural wings against a painted perspective backcloth, these sets formed a permanent background to the ballet, bringing it nearer to the kind of theatre situation that we know today.

After a time the fixed architectural setting seemed very boring; and it was another Italian, Niccolo Sabbatini, who was mainly responsible for evolving various methods of scene change. One was based on the Graeco-Roman *perioktoi*, a three-sided vertical structure that could be revolved to reveal a different scene; then there was a system by which two-sided painted screens could be drawn over to hide the permanent wing structure. A method was invented for changing the backcloth, which was divided into strips or shutters that could be turned or drawn aside to reveal another scene behind. Flying scenery had not then been invented, although a very important factor in the Renaissance theatre was the development of machines for various effects, especially the painted cloud effects often used in conjunction with triumphal cars for the ascent and descent of deities—the usual apotheosis of operas and ballets. Stage lighting at this period was still very primitive. The general practice was to place candles behind bottles of water, tinted with chemicals for colour effects, which intensified the illumination.

All these developments in stagecraft naturally gave far greater scope to the designer and during the late sixteenth and the early seventeenth centuries Italian designers such as the Parigi brothers, Bernardo Buonatalenti, and Giocomo Torelli da Fano created magnificent spectacles of great ingenuity.

What had been happening in the Courts of Italy and France inspired Inigo Jones in England, where masques were playing an essential role in Court life, though on a more modest scale than in the European centres. During the reign of Charles I, however, a new landmark in design was reached. Like most of his predecessors Inigo Jones was primarily an architect, but he was also a very distinguished artist and what he did for the theatre was created more with a painter's eye than with an architect's eye. His concepts lacked the grandiose approach of those in the Courts of Europe, though this did not mean they lacked anything in the way of imagination, ingenuity or visual beauty. In fact Inigo Jones must be considered as the father of stage design in the form that we know today. He was lucky to work with writers such as Ben Jonson, Davenant, and Daniel, and his work for the dance was to have a profound effect on the eventual crystallization of ballet as an integrated art form rather than as a mere adjunct of drama or opera. His designs inspired artists for many centuries; his Night set for Davenant's *Luminalia* of 1638, for instance, could well have been designed for the second act of a Romantic ballet such as *Giselle* two centuries later.

In France during the seventeenth century masques continued in much the same pattern.

They were still based mainly on allegorical subjects, and the dancing was principally performed by members of the Court in a more theatrical version of the social dances of the time; often the king would appear in the 'Grand Ballet' for the apotheosis. But once Louis XIV established the Académie Royal de Danse in 1661, dancing became professional and ballet moved from the confines of the Court to the public theatre. This opened up new vistas for the designer and although the opera-ballet form remained practically unchanged, with costumes principally adapted from contemporary Court dress, great ingenuity was shown by designers such as Henri Gissey and later by the greatest of them all, Jean Berain, who for over thirty years was principal designer for Louis XIV's Court entertainments.

Since ballet is about dancing, it stands to reason that the design of dresses is inevitably governed by the change and development of dance techniques. During the reign of Louis XV steps of elevation were used extensively, which in 1730 led to the great ballerina Marie Camargo shortening her skirts to give greater freedom of movement. Camargo's rival Marie Sallé discarded trappings such as panniers and petticoats, and danced in a flimsy muslin dress with her hair flowing out behind; she seems to have been the forerunner of Isadora Duncan in this century. Then the famous ballet master Jean Georges Noverre, in his *Lettres sur la Danse et les Ballets*, strongly condemned all the old conventions, not only in ballet production but in costume—particularly the mask which was frequently worn up to the mid-eighteenth century. The reforms that Noverre suggested can be seen in some of the designs by Louis Boquet, who succeeded Jean Baptiste Martin as principal designer at the Paris Opéra. Boquet's sets also have greater simplicity, elegance and a lightness that contrasts happily with the more monumental structures of his predecessors.

In Italy the Renaissance form of elaborate presentation continued with ever-increasing magnificence through the seventeenth and eighteenth centuries. Two Italian families dominated the stage not only in Italy but in other European centres, especially Vienna which was to become the principal rival of Paris. Giovanni Burnacini and his son Lodovici created spectacles which made great use of machines and effects. But from 1680 until 1778, Europe was dominated by the Bibiena family: Giovanni Bibiena, his sons Ferdinando and Francesco, grandsons Antonio and Guiseppi, great-grandsons Alessandro and Carlo. The work of this family brought architectural splendour in the theatre to a height never attained before or since, although there were two other designers of importance during the eighteenth century—Gian Piranese and Pietro Gonzago.

1: JACQUES PATIN: *Ballet comique de la Reine*; chor., Beaujoyeux; first given at the Salle du Petit Bourbon, Paris, 1581.

2: JEAN BERAIN: *Le Triomphe de l'amour*; music, Lully; chor., Beauchamp and Pécour; first given at the Château de St.-Germain-en-Laye, 1681.

3: INIGO JONES: *Luminalia* (set, scene 1, Night); masque devised by Sir William Davenant, London, 1638.

4: FERDINANDO GALLI BIBIENA: architectural drawing for a stage set, early eighteenth century.

5: ALESSANDRO SANQUIRICO: *Elerz e Zulmida* (set); chor., Luigi Henry; first given at Teatro alla Scala, Milan, 1826.

6: PIERRE CICERI: *La Sylphide* (set, Act 1); music, Schneitzhoeffer; costumes, Lami; chor., P. Taglioni; first given at the Paris Opéra, 1832.

Over four centuries ballet had gradually become an integrated art form, although the subjects—from classical or Oriental tragedy to pastoral comedy—remained pretty well unchanged. But with the beginning of the nineteenth century the twilight of the gods was at hand. With the Romantic era and the interest in the novels of Walter Scott, the former gods were replaced by supernatural beings such as fairies, naiads, elves and wilis. In France the master of scenic design was Pierre Ciceri, principal designer at the Paris Opéra from 1809, who launched ballet on new flights of imagination with *La Sylphide* in 1832, reaching possibly the greatest height of Romanticism with *Giselle* eight years later. After that nearly every ballet—whether based on Scott or those medieval or Oriental subjects of the Romantic novel—had its woodland or lakeside act, the natural habitat of these supernaturals who tormented, or became enamoured of, the mortal characters. Eugène Lami, and later Paul Lormier, clothed these spirits in ethereal net or tarlatan just-below-knee-length skirts, that gave even greater freedom for elevation, turns, batterie, attitudes and arabesques of the developing dance technique. The master of costumes for the more mortal characters was Hippolyte LeComte.

With the Romantic era Paris became the centre of dance. In Milan the monumental type of production persisted, especially in the work of Alessandro Sanquirico who, in ballets mainly choreographed by Salvatore Viganò, designed sets of architectural splendour as well as romantic cave and mountain landscapes—which may have inspired Ciceri since he was sent to Milan to study Italian stagecraft. Certainly there was a period in the mid-nineteenth century when the Romantic ballet held sway in Italy, undoubtedly due to the fact that the greatest ballerina of the period, Marie Taglioni, came from there. Later, Romanticism gave way to elaborate dance spectacles related to social problems, patriotic fervour, and the glorification of recent scientific and industrial achievements. These were mainly devised by Luigi Manzotti and designed by Alfredo Edel, the most famous being *Excelsior, Amor* and *Sport.* Some of Manzotti's works were presented at the Empire Theatre in London where the designer, from 1887 until 1914, was C. Wilhelm. His costumes were charming and inventive; they remain the perfect example of the kind of design prevalent at the turn of the century.

Unfortunately the Romantic ballet, which brought the art to new pinnacles of imagination during the mid-nineteenth century, descended to a cliché in the last three decades. The sets were usually put in the hands of craftsmen and scene-builders rather than artists. The ballet dresses were mainly variations on those originally created by Lami with merely a change of ornament or decoration to imply the time or place of a particular work; the male costume had similar

7: C. WILHELM: *Les Papillons* (costume for Adeline Genée); given at the Empire Theatre, London, *c. 1900.*

8: ALFREDO EDEL: *Excelsior* (1910 prod.); music, Marenco; chor., Manzotti; first given at Teatro alla Scala, Milan, 1881.

variations on the basic tights, shorts, doublet or jerkin. Although ballet had become integrated as an art form, by the end of the nineteenth century the designing of it had virtually returned to square one.

But just as the two schools of dance—the French school from Paris, the Italian school from Milan—moved into St. Petersburg to combine with the existing Russian school and form the Imperial Russian Ballet School, the design of ballet there was also influenced by these two schools. The conventions of the French Romantic ballet merged with the elaborate presentations of Italy in the design of the great three-act ballets, mainly by Petipa and Ivanov, at the Maryinsky Theatre in St. Petersburg. For instance, the sets by A.M. Shiskov and the dresses by I.A. Vsevolozhsky, for the first production of the Petipa/Tchaikovsky *La Belle au*

*bois dormant* in 1890, appear to be working on completely different levels. Apart from anything else the principal dancers often paid little heed to the designs but wore their own costumes, regardless of the fact that they might be totally at variance with the theme of a particular work. It was against this design malpractice that a number of intellectuals in St. Petersburg started to revolt. In other parts of Europe there were other forces at work that were to revolutionize the entire concept of stage presentation. All of this was eventually to bring the designer of ballet up to the same level of importance as the choreographer, composer and dancer. For four centuries the designer (architect and dressmaker) existed to decorate or supply a suitable background to ballet; in the twentieth century, design became an organic part of the whole conception.

At the turn of the century, two men—Edward Gordon Craig and Adolphe Appia—were the driving force that was to change the whole concept of design in the theatre. Although the ballet was never their major concern, their theories were to open up new relationships between the player/dancer and space, lighting, setting and costumes. Craig, in fact, spoke rather vehemently against the dancer: 'I do not hold, that with the renaissance of the dance comes the renaissance of the ancient art of the theatre, for I do not hold that the ideal dancer is the perfect expression of all that is most perfect in movement.' A strange statement indeed from one who was so emotionally involved with the great dance pioneer, Isadora Duncan. Craig was up in arms against the former realism in the theatre; he wanted it replaced by symbolism. He considered that the art of the theatre lay 'not in the actors, the stage setting or in the dance but is composed of elements which make up the play of the actor, the drama, the setting and the dance; of gesture which is the soul of acting; of words which are the body of the play; of lines and colours, which are the very existence of the stage decoration; of rhythm which is the essence of the dance.' Craig felt that the finished production must be a harmonious combination of gesture, word, dance and image. Although these theories were mainly intended to be applied to drama productions there is no doubt that, directly or indirectly, they were to influence the whole attitude towards the making of ballet in the twentieth century.

Adolphe Appia was really the first person to make stage lighting a living art rather than merely a means of illumination, as it had been before the invention of electricity. Like Craig, Appia believed that stage settings should be three-dimensional instead of being a painted cloth, and that lighting must reveal the three-dimensional nature of the set as well as that of the player or dancer performing within it. More than anything he felt that the arrangement and ordering of the stage in all its detail is to be found contained in the music; his theories about this are examined in his famous book, *Die Musik und die Inscenierung*, which revolutionized the production of Wagner operas. 'Light', he wrote, 'is no more the mere possibility of seeing than music is synonymous with sound.' Appia's work evolved even further when he collaborated with Jacques Dalcroze at Hellerau. Through working with the dancers at that famous school he developed his theories in which purity of line, order and measure combining in a rhythmic space are interpreted by the living body. It was due to Appia's pioneering work that, later in the century, the lighting designer took on a vital role in stage production, often taking over from the more conventional methods of stage design. So within a few hours of the twentieth century being born a new horizon for design was opened up. To the symbolism of Craig's setting and Appia's lighting was added the symbolic use of colour, entirely due to the introduction of painters to the theatre and especially to ballet.

Since the work of Craig and Appia was becoming known in the main theatre centres of Europe, it was undoubtedly observed by a wealthy Muscovite manufacturer, S. Mamontov, who was sponsoring a new attack against realism—mainly on opera productions in Moscow—at the same time as Stanislavsky was waging the same campaign for drama at his Moscow Art Theatre. In his belief that stage design must be more than just a background for the performer, Mamontov employed easel painters such as Vasnetzov and Korovine to design his productions. Mamontov also sponsored an art journal *Mir Iskusstva* (*The World of Art*), founded by St. Petersburg artists Alexandre Benois and Léon Bakst in 1899. This journal, edited by Serge Diaghilev, was the organ of a group of intellectuals that jokingly called themselves 'The Pickwickians', all deeply involved with artistic reforms—in painting and sculpture,

later expanding to music, literature and ballet. The most immediate effect of this group's achievement was that the painter became involved in the creation of ballet, on a level equal to that of the composer, choreographer and dancer. The focus which for four hundred years had been on Milan and Paris, moved to St. Petersburg in the early years of this century. As a result of all these forces at work, ballet, together with other arts, was poised on the brink of a new renaissance.

9: EDWARD GORDON CRAIG: design for a scene, 1907.

10: ADOLPH APPIA: *Orphée* (set); music, Gluck; chor., Jacques Dalcroze; given at Hellerau, Switzerland, 1906.

# The Russian influence

The course of history can change radically, perhaps owing to some seemingly minor incident (the bullet that killed Franz Ferdinand at Sarajevo in 1914 is a case in point), or perhaps owing to the vision of one person or a small group. It is doubtful whether, at the time, the St. Petersburg group responsible for the magazine *Mir Iskusstva* could have envisaged just how much the reforms for which they were fighting would change the whole course of the arts, ballet most of all. Of those in the group it was Alexandre Benois, a painter with great historical knowledge, who alone had a love of ballet, although the rest—artists such as Bakst, Korovine, Serov and so on—shared an intense love of theatre. In the early years Diaghilev's interests lay mostly with music and painting; it was a young dancer and ballet master at the Maryinsky Theatre, Michel Fokine, who was to change his mind. Fokine became involved with the group when it was realized that his ideas for ballet reform were similar to theirs.

That liberated American dancer, Isadora Duncan, left a deep impression on Fokine when she appeared in St. Petersburg in 1904. The fact that Duncan discarded conventional ballet costume, dancing bare-footed in flowing draperies to give her body complete freedom of movement, made Fokine realize that the time had come for dance to be freed from past constrictions. In the same year he happened to read Longus's *Daphnis and Chloë* which inspired him to write a scenario for a two-act ballet, which he submitted to the Imperial Theatres. It was rejected; but his explanatory notes, which included suggestions for ballet reform, were to determine entirely new relationships between thematic idea, choreography and dance, music and design. 'Dance', he wrote, 'should express the whole epoch to which the subject of the ballet belongs . . .'; 'The harmony which these dances must have with the theme, period, and the style, demands a new view-point in the matter of decoration and costume . . .'; 'In

place of the traditional dualism, the ballet must have complete unity of expression, a unity which is made up of a harmonious blending of the three elements—music, painting and the plastic art.'

In fact Fokine was saying about ballet much the same thing that Gordon Craig had said about reforms in theatre production. The first example of these theories at work came with Fokine's *Le Pavillon d'Armide*, a ballet developed from a student performance at the Maryinsky, which Benois designed as well as writing the scenario. Although it could not be said that this work, in which an eighteenth-century viscount dreams of a tapestry coming to life, advanced the theories of combined forces to any great extent, it was a start. Certainly there was a harmony between Benois' designs based on baroque masques, Tcherepnine's score, and Fokine's declarations about the blending of all three elements. There was this same blending when Benois and Fokine again combined in a ballet, also originally made for a student performance, that became the very essence of nineteenth-century Romanticism—*Chopiniana* (later renamed *Les Sylphides*).

Meanwhile Diaghilev had been arranging exhibitions of contemporary Russian painting in St. Petersburg, and an important exhibition of Russian portraits at the Tauride Palace in 1905; the following year he organized an exhibition of Russian painting in Paris, the first of its kind ever seen outside Russia, and many of the artists were to play an important part in ballet. The success of this led to concerts of Russian music in 1907; the following year Diaghilev brought Chaliapine to the Paris Opéra in Moussorgsky's *Boris Godounov*. The way was clear for an onslaught on Western Europe of the Russian art that was to combine all these arts, namely ballet. The Imperial Russian Ballet, under the direction of Diaghilev, opened at the Théâtre du Châtelet, Paris, on 19 May 1909; this and subsequent seasons brought ballet and the allied arts into the twentieth century.

In the integration of elements that make the composite art of ballet, the involvement of the easel painter was the greatest step forward in the visual impact of the whole. During those early Diaghilev seasons, what impressed Western Europe most from the design aspect was the symbolic use of colour. That colour could bring a new dramatic meaning and poetic suggestiveness was never shown more clearly than in the ballets designed by Léon Bakst. He was a master at building up colour, or subtly introducing it, to create an effect which worked in perfect accord with the nature of the choreography and the music. In this way he created an exoticism that stunned the West, in dance dramas such as *Schéhérazade*, *Le Dieu bleu* and *Thamar*. He had an impeccable eye for creating just the right atmosphere, whether it be the rather stark Victorian débutante's bedroom of *Le Spectre de la rose*; the anteroom of blue walls surmounted by a black and gold dado, for *Le Carnaval*; the lush Greek landscape of *L'Après-midi d'un faune* or *Daphnis and Chloë*; the hazy enclosed garden of *Jeux*. In Bakst's last work for Diaghilev there was a return to baroque grandeur with a revival of the Petipa/Tchaikovsky classic *The Sleeping Princess*, in 1921. There was also an unerring rightness about the dresses Bakst designed—their silhouettes and use of materials—which caused the dancer to move in a way that accorded with the style or period of the piece.

Russian painters changed the whole attitude towards ballet design; they were to dominate the Diaghilev repertory until 1917. As well as Benois and Bakst designing ballets during those first Paris seasons, there was another painter, Nicholas Roerich, who evoked a rather different geographical and ethnic aspect of Russia. His designs for the Polovtsian dances from *Prince Igor* evoked all the primitive savagery and bleakness of the steppes, the perfect landscape for the frenzied warriors. It was this Fokine ballet that sealed the success of Diaghilev's first Paris season; Western audiences had never seen anything like it. Later Roerich designed a more mystical, though equally primitive, landscape for Nijinsky's *Le Sacre du printemps*.

In 1910 the course of twentieth-century music was determined when Stravinsky's score for Fokine's *L'Oiseau de feu* was first heard; Alexander Golovine's designs reflected the fairytale magic of the music. The next year Stravinsky wrote the score for a work that fully realized the true blending of elements towards which Fokine and his associates had been working. Never before had these elements—book and design by Benois, music by Stravinsky, choreography by Fokine—become so perfectly interlocked as in *Petrushka*. Benois' designs for the happenings during Butterweek Fair in St.

11: MICHEL LARIONOV: *Le Renard* (set); music, Stravinsky; chor., Nijinska; first given by the Diaghilev Ballet at Théâtre National de l'Opéra, Paris, 1922.

Petersburg are the perfect amalgam of realism and symbolism.

It is possible that by 1914 Diaghilev felt things were sinking into a rut, that some new injection was needed; so on Benois' advice he journeyed to Russia to see the work of a group of modernistic painters practising in Moscow. He found Natalia Goncharova and her husband Mikhail Larionov; their work was to form the bridge between the early, more traditional, Russian painters and the modern European painters who dominated the final twelve years of the Diaghilev Ballet. Both artists were influenced by primitive peasant art and Goncharova's designs for Fokine's *Le Coq d'or* (1914), inspired by early Russian chapbooks, brought a glow of rich colour to the stage that had not been seen before and seldom since; in complete contrast, but no less stunning, was the starkness of her peasant wedding in Nijinska's *Les Noces*, nine years later, in which the colour was reduced to earthy monochrome. This same form of Russian peasant art inspired Larionov in his design of Massine's first ballets, *Midnight Sun* (1915) and *Contes Russes* (1917), which had the sophisticated naïveté of children's paintings. Although after 1917 the 'Russian-ness' largely disappeared from the whole ballet concept, the world of art owes everything to the vision of that small St. Petersburg band of intellectuals who, in the early years of the century, laid the foundation for ballet, with its collective of arts on the highest level, to become a major theatre art in a manner unknown in the previous four centuries of its existence.

Diaghilev had been based in Europe for so many years (his last trip to Russia was in 1914) that it was natural, since he had always shown an interest in modern painters, for him eventually to turn to the world capital of creative arts—Paris. War and revolution had cut him off from Russia where, apart from a brief post-revolution blaze which brought Constructavism to the theatre, design reverted to the kind of realism from which the original St. Petersburg group left Russia to escape. The poet Jean Cocteau, lover of the avant-garde and of ballet since the 1909 season, guided Diaghilev towards the Cubist movement and its founder Pablo Picasso. Cocteau had an idea for a rather satirical ballet about characters in a fairground booth, that he felt might work with the Cubist manifesto. Picasso was interested since, at that period in the middle of the 1914–18 war, he was anxious to promote Cubism by relating it to the theatre. Diaghilev was also anxious to involve his young choreographer, Leonide Massine, in modern art forms. The result of this collaboration—choreography by Massine, book by Cocteau, music by Eric Satie, design by Picasso—was *Parade*, first given in Paris at the Théâtre du Châtelet on 18 May 1917. It had a very mixed reception—the more traditional audience was horrified; the younger audience, especially the modern artists who had previously shunned ballet as too reactionary, was delighted. Really important was the fact that modern art had become totally integrated with ballet's other elements. Picasso's towering Cubist structure for the two rival managers became virtually the first instance of choreographed sculpture. For *Parade* Diaghilev got Picasso to design a special front-cloth; thereby began a practice that was to continue with most of the creations for the Diaghilev company until 1929, and to a lesser extent after that. The front-cloth was an important development because not only did it form a visual prologue which, together with the overture music, instantly created the style

and atmosphere of the work to follow, but also allowed the easel painter's imagination to work in its rightful territory—the vastly enlarged canvas.

The experience of *Parade* brought a pioneer figure of twentieth-century painting to the theatre, fulfilling his desire to relate art forms to real life; it was also the spur which encouraged other artists, then struggling for greater recognition, to follow his example. The other two major works which Picasso was to design for Diaghilev—*Le Tricorne* (1919) and *Pulcinella* (1920)—were not so heavily related to any particular 'ism', but they provided magnificent examples of how a painter—with his knowledge of simple graphic line, distribution of colour masses, and elimination of all superfluous detail—can create exactly the right climate a particular work might need. Just a few lines on a light ochre back-cloth instantly evoked the burning plains of Andalusia in *Le Tricorne*; brilliant distribution of simple shapes seemed to conjure up even the smell of a Neapolitan backstreet in *Pulcinella*. All this was achieved while still leaving maximum space for dancing.

After 1917 Diaghilev sought his designers from the School of Paris, with just a few notable exceptions. Apart from Picasso, there was André Derain for *La Boutique fantasque* (1919), José-Maria Sert for the opera ballet *Astuces féminines* (1920, but presented as a one-act ballet, *Cimerosiana*, in 1924). In 1921 there was, however, a departure from the modern school when Diaghilev decided to revive the great Maryinsky classic *The Sleeping Princess* at the Alhambra Theatre, London. Bakst's designs were magnificent and the cast included some of the greatest dancers of the century; but the revival failed to draw a public which by then had become acclimatized to one-act works involving modern painters and composers. Although it was a costly failure for Diaghilev, the foundation was laid for the eventual formation of British ballet; it inspired Ninette de Valois, who was in the company, and

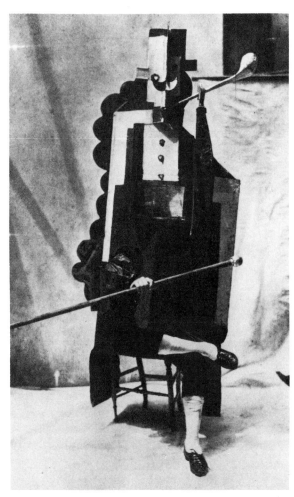

12: PABLO PICASSO: *Parade* (costumes for French and American managers); music, Satie; chor., Massine; first given at Théâtre du Châtelet, Paris, 1917.

twenty-five years later the Petipa/Tchaikovsky classic—with designs by Oliver Messel owing much to Bakst—brought international fame to the Sadler's Wells Ballet.

In addition to artists already mentioned, the list of those used between 1917 and 1929 reads like a history of twentieth-century painting: Henri Matisse (*Le Rossignol*), Marie Laurençin (*Les Biches*), Georges Braque (*Les Fâcheux* and *Zéphyr et Flore*), Juan Gris (*Les Tentations de la bergère*), Maurice Utrillo (*Barabau*), Pedro Pruna (*Les Matelots*), Max Ernst and Joan Miró (*Romeo and Juliet*), André Bauchant (*Apollon musagète*), Giorgio de Chirico (*Le Bal*), Georges Rouault (*Le Fils prodigue*). Most of these artists worked for Diaghilev on the advice of Cocteau and Boris Kochno, who was also responsible for many of the librettos. It must be admitted that while many of these artists created stage pictures of great beauty, a gargantuan exhibition of modern painting, not all of them became totally integrated with the dancing and choreography. But the very fact of using artists of such genius not only enriched the art of ballet at that time, but was to inspire the whole attitude towards design in the theatre.

The fact that Diaghilev brought modern painters

13: JEAN HUGO: *Les Mariés de la Tour Eiffel* (costume design, a photographer); music, Les Six; chor., Borlin; given by Ballets Suédois, Théâtre des Champs-Elysées, Paris, 1921.

14: GIORGIO DI CHIRICO: *Le Bal* (set); music, Rieti; chor., Balanchine; given by the Diaghilev Ballet, Théâtre de Monte-Carlo, 1929.

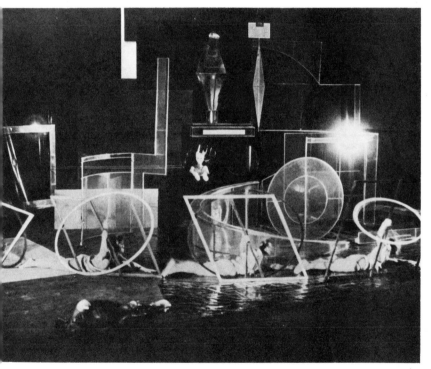

15: NAUM GABO AND ANTOINE PEVSNER: *La Chatte* (prod. picture); music, Sauguet; chor., Balanchine; first given by the Diaghilev Ballet at Théâtre de Monte-Carlo, 1927.

of the Paris School to ballet probably influenced Rolf de Maré, a rich Swedish landowner and art lover, when in 1920 he formed Ballets Suédois around the Swedish dancer and choreographer Jean Borlin. The company only lasted four years but the avant-garde nature of the works, all written by Borlin, was to have a far-reaching effect upon many future projects. It brought the Cubist painter Fernand Léger into ballet with *Skating-Rink* and *La Création du monde* (recounting the creation of man through primitive African art). Then Andrée Parr designed a set in which the dancers moved on different parallel levels for *L'Homme et son désir*, based on a poem by Claudel. Of the many works created for the company the most extraordinary was undoubtedly *Relâche*, designed by Francis Picabia. Its mixture of film projection by René Clair and Eric Satie music, with surrealistic use of various objects, may have overpowered Borlin's choreography, but it was virtually the first instance of what later came to be known as 'multi-media'.

These experiments may have influenced Diaghilev when, in the last years of his life, he turned towards a form then emerging in the Soviet theatre—Constructavism. This form, possibly inspired by the theories of Craig and Appia, discarded the painted set and replaced it with three-dimensional structures of varying material and texture, in which the player/dancer became involved. The first manifestation of this in the Diaghilev repertory came with *La Chatte* in which the designers, Gabo and Pevsner, placed Balanchine's choreographed version of an Aesop fable in a world of geometric shapes constructed of talc, resting on an expanse of shiny black American cloth; the costumes were devised in the same idiom and the reflection of light from these materials created a magical effect. Even closer to Soviet Constructavism were the lathes, work-bench rostrums, moving wheels and pistons of Georgi Yakoulov's design for Massine's *Le Pas d'acier*, which brought ballet into the machine age.

16: FRANCIS PICABIA: *Relâche* (prod. picture); music, Satie; chor., Borlin; first given by Ballets Suédois at Théâtre des Champs-Elysées, Paris, 1924.

17: GEORGES YAKULOV: *Le Pas d'acier* (model of set); music, Prokofiev; chor., Massine; first given by the Diaghilev Ballet at Théâtre Sarah Bernhardt, Paris, 1928.

Constructavism in a more modified form came with Pavel Tchelitchev's designing of *Ode*. It was a multi-media event for which Nicholas Nabokov composed a cantata based on an ode by the eighteenth-century poet Lomonosov. There was an Aristotelian unity in the complete integration of dance, mime, music, choral speech—and light. This was possibly the first time that light was used with such poetic imagination; the pale blue gauzes illuminated from behind created a dreamlike effect. Remarkable false perspective was achieved by having dolls, dressed identically to the dancers, suspended in an inverted 'V'. At the time these three more experimental works did not have any lasting success with the public, but the seeds were sown of a form that was to influence designers, and indeed the whole conception of dance theatre, in later years.

18: PAVEL TCHELITCHEV: *Ode* (set); music, Nabokov; chor., Massine; first given by the Diaghilev Ballet at Théâtre Sarah Bernhardt, Paris, 1928.

There are probably no persons—choreographers and dancers in any field, composers, painters, designers—working in dance theatre today who do not owe what they are doing, and the way that they are doing it, to the achievements of Diaghilev. He died in 1929, his company disbanded, and his traditions were carried on during the thirties by two major companies, Les Ballets Russes de Col. de Basil, and René Blum's Les Ballets de Monte-Carlo.

Without Diaghilev's unerring taste and innate sense of fitness, which caused him to make famous painters rethink their designs until the right one was achieved, many works lacked the integration they would have had in his time. In the early years of the de Basil company, however, Massine—who had been schooled by Diaghilev—applied the same tenets in the use of modern painters for his ballets. Possibly the happiest example of this was *Jeux d'enfants* for which the Spanish painter Joan Miró created a surreal child's world of toys and games in bright clear colours. An important development in Massine's work during the early thirties was the symphonic ballet, with known symphonies being transmuted into dance. The first of these, *Les Présages* to Tchaikovsky's fifth symphony, had turbulent designs by the surrealistic painter André Masson, reflecting the theme of the work—man's fight with destiny. Of these early symphonics ballets it was *Symphonie fantastique*, to Berlioz' music of the same name, which established Christian Bérard as a designer of great importance. There was a grandeur of conception in the incidents from a Romantic poet's opium dream that was matched by Massine's choreography. Bérard, whose first work for ballet had been Balanchine's elegant *Cotillion* (1932), was to have great influence on ballet design in the post-war years. A notable dramatic work by David Lichine brought Oliver Messel, a very distinguished designer of revues and musicals, to ballet proper; his designs for *Francesca da Rimini* brought the

Italian Renaissance vibrantly alive. Then there was Jean Hugo who, in 1924, had designed a historic production of *Roméo et Juliette* for Les Soirées de Paris; black predominated, with the set and dresses outlined and decorated in simple, mainly white, graphic lines. For de Basil, eleven years later, Hugo's simple colour masses, with elimination of all superfluous detail, brought a remarkable fairy-tale quality to Nijinska's *Cent baisers*.

In the early years of René Blum's Ballet de Monte-Carlo, Fokine returned to choreography. His best work was *L'Épreuve d'amour* for which André Derain designed an exquisite chinoiserie set and dresses which worked perfectly with the Mozart music. Also for this company, Cassandre designed his first ballet, Balanchine's *Aubade*; later he was to design a number of works, mainly using architectural perspective, for the Paris Opéra. Blum's company was caught in America on the outbreak of war; it remained there, never returning to Europe, as Ballet Russe de Monte-Carlo. For that first season in New York Massine collaborated with the foremost surrealistic artist, Salvador Dali, on *Bacchanale*; based on the hallucinations of the eccentric Ludwig of Bavaria, danced to the Venusberg music from Wagner's *Tannhäuser*, the whole idea was eminently suited to surrealism. Massine returned to Henri Matisse, with whom he had worked for Diaghilev, for *L'Étrange Farandole* (originally entitled *Rouge et noir*), and again realized the simplicity of line and colour that worked so well for symphonic ballets (in this case, Dmitri Shostakovitch's first symphony). Although there had been considerable pioneering in America during the thirties—such as Mordkin's company at the Metropolitan Opera, Catherine Littlefield's Philadelphia Ballet, and others—it was the tours of Ballet Russe de Monte-Carlo that were mainly responsible for igniting an explosion of dance that was to take many new and varied forms.

The thirties saw the beginnings of ballet in

England, but were it not for the fact that two ladies—Marie Rambert and Ninette de Valois—had both been associated with the Diaghilev company, it is doubtful whether British ballet would ever have got off the ground in the way that it did. Again it was one of those seemingly minor events that sparked off the whole thing. Marie Rambert was asked to provide a short ballet for an intimate revue, *Riverside Nights*. She had in her school a young dancer, Frederick Ashton, whom she felt had choreographic talent; she also had a young painter friend, Sophie Fedorovitch. The result of their first collaboration was *A Tragedy of Fashion* at the Lyric Theatre, Hammersmith, on 6 June 1926. The Ashton/Fedorovitch partnership was to produce some of the key works in the formation of the British repertory.

Since Rambert's company, the Ballet Club (later Ballet Rambert) functioned mainly on the tiny stage of the Mercury Theatre, or other stages not much larger, the design had to be kept very simple. There was a minimum of detail in Fedorovitch's sets and dresses and the colour range was equally limited: *Les Masques* was very chic in black, white, and grey; *Valentine's Eve* was all in shades of plum; while for Andrée Howard's *La Fête étrange* Fedorovitch, with the same economy, created a poetic glacial landscape for the party in Fournier's novel on which the ballet was based. Fedorovitch worked so closely with choreographers that sets and dresses gradually evolved as a ballet progressed through studio rehearsals; seldom was there a finished design until after a work was completed. A number of other artists had their first chance to design ballets in those early years, among the most notable being William Chappell (many works for Ashton, Antony Tudor's *Lysistrata*, de Valois' *Bar au Folies-Bergère*); Hugh Stevenson (Tudor's *The Planets*, *Jardin aux lilas*, *Gala Performance*); and John Armstrong (*Façade*).

The company which Ninette de Valois founded in 1931, the Vic-Wells Ballet (later The Sadler's Wells Ballet), emerged from a group of dancers originally assembled in 1928 to appear in plays and operas at the Old Vic; there were also occasional ballet evenings. Some of the original Vic-Wells repertory came from the Camargo Society, which gave occasional performances with the aim of promoting British ballets and painters; it gave the company its first major work, de Valois' *Job*, for which Gwendolen Raverat based her designs on William Blake. From the start de Valois, like Rambert, realized from working with Diaghilev the importance of involving contemporary painters in ballet. In the beginning it was artists such as Vanessa Bell (*Pomona*), John Armstrong (*Birthday of Oberon*), and Edward Burra (*Rio Grande*) who got their first chance of working in the theatre. After the company was based at

19: SOPHIE FEDOROVITCH: *Les Masques* (set); music, Poulenc; chor., Ashton; given by The Ballet Club, the Mercury Theatre, London, 1933.

20: MCKNIGHT KAUFFER: *Checkmate* (prod. picture); music, Bliss; chor., de Valois; given by the Sadler's Wells Ballet, Théâtre des Champs-Elysées, Paris, 1937.

1: SOPHIE FEDOROVITCH: *La Fête étrange* (Sadler's Wells Theatre Ballet prod.); music, Fauré; chor., Howard; first given by London Ballet at the Arts Theatre, London, 1940. (Photo: Houston Rogers)

2: KENNETH ROWELL: *Le Baiser de la fée* (set, scene 4); music, Stravinsky; chor., MacMillan; given by the Royal Ballet at the Royal Opera House, Covent Garden, 1960. (Photo: Donald Southern)

Sadler's Wells Theatre in 1934, de Valois' greatest successes were: *The Haunted Ballroom*, designed by Motley (a notable team of stage designers); *The Rake's Progress* with Rex Whistler's designs based on Hogarth; and *Checkmate* for which the famous poster artist, McKnight Kauffer, achieved a sinister geometric landscape for a deadly game of chess. In 1935 Ashton left Rambert to become principal choreographer of the Vic-Wells Ballet; his collaboration with Fedorovitch resulted in two outstanding works in those pre-war years, *Le Baiser de la fée* and *Horoscope*. Although Fedorovitch was to remain Ashton's principal advisor until her death in 1953, she did not design all his ballets; Cecil Beaton brought an almost Fedorovitch-like simplicity of line and colour to *Apparitions*, while Berners most wittily designed and composed the score of *A Wedding Bouquet* to words by Gertrude Stein.

In those pre-war years ballet was really only appreciated by a devoted following in London. With the wartime evacuation of London and the closing of theatres, The Sadler's Wells Ballet, as it had then become, was forced to tour the English provinces, as were Ballet Rambert and other dance companies then being formed. This touring—of cities, army camps, factories and so on—was responsible for building up the vast audience for ballet that England still has. As Sadler's Wells Theatre had been bombed, the company gave regular London seasons at the New Theatre where the audience consisted mainly of those on leave from the armed forces. The war years were very productive in many respects. Easel painters designed two Ashton works: Graham Sutherland for *The Wanderer*, John Piper for *The Quest*. Edward Burra returned to ballet with *Miracle in the Gorbals* choreographed by the company's principal dancer, Robert Helpmann (who in 1942 had written his first piece, *Comus*, designed by Oliver Messel, his first for the company). Helpmann's most important work, however, was *Hamlet*, a surreal dance drama based on Shakespeare's play which brought to the forefront a most important designer, Leslie Hurry, whose Blake-like vision and bold use of colour was imaginative and beautiful.

By the end of the war in 1944, Diaghilev had been dead only fifteen years, but everything of any importance that had happened in ballet had been inspired by his taste, and his unique knowledge of how all the arts can work together to the greater glory of one art—ballet.

23: EDWARD BURRA: *Miracle in the Gorbals* (set); music, Bliss; chor., Helpmann; first given by the Sadler's
Wells Ballet at Princes Theatre, London, 1944.

24: OSBERT LANCASTER: *Pineapple Poll* (prod. picture, scene 1); music Sullivan (arr. Mackerras); chor.,
Cranko; first given by the Sadler's Wells Theatre Ballet at Sadler's Wells Theatre, London, 1951. (Photo: de Marney)

# The world explodes in dance

The immediate post-war years saw the beginning of what was to become a worldwide dance explosion, the central force shifting between Paris, New York, and London. Design focused first on Paris, where two former associates of Diaghilev, Boris Kochno and Jean Cocteau, joined forces with the painter Christian Bérard. In opposition to the official attitude then prevailing at the Paris Opéra they decided to form a company around the young dancers and progressive painters then emerging. From 1941–4 Irène Lidova had been organizing occasional performances choreographed by two young dancers, Janine Charrat and Roland Petit; the latter created a

notable work, *Les Forains*. The official opening of Ballets des Champs-Elysées, in the theatre after which it was named, was 12 October 1945. 'All that was left to us of the unforgettable Phoenix, Serge Diaghilev, were his ashes' wrote Jean Cocteau. 'But we know the myth, this Phoenix died to spring up again from the ashes. Boris Kochno, who assisted Diaghilev in his work, is now organizing a veritable festival of youth and dancing. Once again we see him grouping the painters, the choreographers, the dancers. Around Roland Petit, the dispersed quicksilver reassembles itself and forms a block, which vibrates and sparkles. The Phoenix meditated upon its

25: ALEXANDRE CASSANDRE: *Le Chavalier et la damoiselle* (set); music, Gaubert; chor., Lifar; given by the Ballet de Théâtre National de l'Opéra, Paris, 1941. (Photo: Lido)

26

substance, re-organized its great soul and its multi-coloured plumage, in the secret fire.' Indeed it really did seem as though Diaghilev was being reborn in this company of wonderful dancers, brilliant ideas and host of designers. First of all came Petit's *Les Forains*, another ballet about circus people, which Bérard designed with masterly economy. In a black space the only props were a cart, a few poles to make a fit-up stage, and a red curtain. With imaginative lighting, nothing more was needed to create the right feeling of desolation on the outskirts of a town where an itinerant troupe would perform. Other known artists who designed for that first season were Jean Hugo, who bought sun-splashed classical simplicity to Petit's *Les Amours de Jupiter*, and Marie Laurençin who gave Petit's *Le Déjeuner sur l'herbe* a pastel meridian haze. The as yet unknown designers included: André Beaurepaire whose black and white set made an exciting background to sparkling chic dresses in Marcel Berger's *Concert de danse*; Jean-Denis Malclés who gave Petit's *La Fiancée du diable* a real sense of Romantic Gothic melodrama; Antoni Clavé whose sense of form and rich colour was first seen in Ana Nevada's *Los Caprichos*; and Pierre Roy who, in Charrat's *Jeu de cartes*, did for cards what McKnight Kauffer had done for chess in de Valois' ballet. The blown-up photographs by Brassai seemed to evoke the smell of nocturnal Paris backstreets for Petit's *Le Rendez-vous*.

Later seasons introduced more ideas such as Petit's *Le Jeune Homme et la mort*, based on an idea by Cocteau; Georges Wakhevitch created a realistic studio for this tale of a young painter who is so ill-treated by his girlfriend that he hangs himself. The studio walls fly away and Death (the girl in a long white evening dress) leads the boy away over the Paris rooftops. Then there was Bérard again, and a red plush, gold-fringed trapeze suspended in a stark landscape, for the Sphinx to confront the questioning Oedipus in Lichine's *La Reconte*. American designer Tom Keogh brought fresh colours and exciting new forms to Milloss's *Portrait of Don Quixote* and Babilée's *Tyl Eulenspiegel*. Roland Petit broke away from the company in 1948 and formed his own company, Ballets de Paris. This company created a similarly remarkable collection of original works, the most notable of which were designed by Léonor Fini (*Les Demoiselles de la nuit*), Clavé (*Carmen* and *Deuil en vingt-quatre heures*), and Jean Carzou (*Le Loup*).

Both these French companies were to have a tremendous effect on the whole approach to ballet-making everywhere. Les Ballets des Champs-Elysées was the first foreign company to visit London after the war, and in 1946 it provided a shot in the arm to the rather war-weary British ballet. Just before the company arrived, however,

26: CHRISTIAN BERARD: *Les Forains* (set); music, Sauguet; chor., Petit; given by Ballets des Champs-Elysées at Théâtre Sarah Bernhardt, Paris, 1945.

27: BRASSAI: *Le Rendez-vous* (scene 1); music, Kosma; chor., Petit; given by Ballets des Champs-Elysées at Théâtre Sarah Bernhardt, Paris, 1945. (Photo: Lipnitzky)

Frederick Ashton created his first work, *Symphonic Variations*, for the Sadler's Wells Ballet (soon to become the Royal Ballet) after its move to the Royal Opera House, Covent Garden. For this Sophie Fedorovitch, who always claimed Bérard as her main inspiration, designed a masterly set with fine black calligraphic lines swirling on a lily-of-the-valley leaf-green backcloth; against this the six dancers, all in white, moved in a celestial relationship with the César Franck music. Later, Italian painter Lila de Nobili designed Ashton's three-act *Ondine* with beautifully muted romanticism. These and the French artists kindled the imagination of a new generation.

GEORGES WAKHEVITCH: *Le Jeune Homme et la mort* (Babilée and Philippart); music, Bach; prod., Cocteau; chor., Petit; given by Ballets des Champs-Elysées at Théâtre des Champs-Elysées, Paris, 1946. (Photo: Lido)

The first notable change came when Kenneth MacMillan discovered Nicholas Georgiadis, a promising Greek student at the Slade School of Art, and invited him to design his first commissioned work, *Danses concertantes*, for the Sadler's Wells Theatre Ballet in 1955; in the same year they collaborated again in *House of Birds*, and were to work together on many ballets through the years. Up to that point it must be admitted that ballet design in Britain had tended to be very Anglo-Saxon in its restraint. Georgiadis' rich sense of colour and form, mainly inspired by Mediterranean antiquity, was to bring a more positive attitude to design; and later, when he

became co-director of the theatre design department at the Slade with Peter Snow, they were mainly responsible for guiding a new generation. The first work of some of these students—such as Yolanda Sonnabend (*The Blue Rose*), Philip Prowse (*Diversions*), Derek Jarman (*Jazz Calendar*), Ian Spurling (*Seven Deadly Sins*), Pamela Marr (*Rashamon*) all for the Royal Ballet; Peter Docharty (*Ephemeron*) for Western Theatre Ballet; Elizabeth Dalton (*The Taming of the Shrew*) for Stuttgart—was responsible for them later becoming international names. Not only the Slade but also the Central School of Art and Design has produced artists who have enriched ballet. Peter Farmer, first known for designing Jack Carter's *Agrionia* for London Dance Theatre, went on to design Romantic classics in many countries, as well as more modern works such as *Stages* for London Contemporary Dance Theatre. Ralph Koltai, whose designs have what is best described as stylized realism, is at his best in ballets that have a dramatic theme—mainly in works by Norman Morrice for Ballet Rambert. Another designer whose main work has been for Ballet Rambert, although she has an international reputation, is Nadine Baylis. Her abstract forms— arrangement of shimmering gauzes, plain surfaces, sculptural shapes—create the space and perfect atmosphere for works by Morrice or Glen Tetley. It was Sophie Fedorovitch's *Symphonic Variations* that first fired the imagination of Baylis. Similarly, she seldom puts anything on paper as a finished design until a ballet is completed, but works closely with the choreographer, dancers and lighting designer during the whole creative process. In fact, due to Appia's pioneering of light as a living art in the early years of the century, the lighting designer has become a vital element in the creation of dance works. The high standard of presentation, especially of contemporary works in Britain, is largely due to the imagination of lighting designers such as John B. Read, David Hersey, John Anderton, Richard Casswell and others.

Several artists, not trained at the aforementioned two London schools, have made very valuable contributions to the visual aspect of the British dance scene. Amongst them are two Australians: Kenneth Rowell (earliest works for Walter Gore including *Winter Night*, *Carte blanche*; for MacMillan *Laiderette*, *Baiser de la fée* among others) and Barry Kay (Peter Darrell's *The Prisoners*, MacMillan's *Anastasia* among others). From South Africa, Peter Cazalet, a dancer who originally studied architecture, has brought a new look to classics such as *Swan Lake*, *La Sylphide* or *Napoli*, principally for Scottish Ballet. All these designers and several more were responsible for the fact that from the early sixties the focus switched to London rather than Paris. Which does

not mean to say that there were few interesting
things happening in the rest of Europe. In
Germany, for instance, Jürgen Rose was
responsible for some splendid designs for works
mainly by John Cranko (notably *Romeo and
Juliet, Onegin, Poème de l'extase*) presented by the
Stuttgart Ballet. In Holland the
dancer/painter/sculptor Toer van Schayk brought
his skills to many fine works by Rudi van Dantzig
for the Dutch National Ballet; their first,
*Monument for a Dead Boy*, brought choreography
and abstract sets together in a very powerful
psychological study of the effect that a disrupted
home can have on the emotions of a young boy.
Later van Schayk was to design the ballets he also
choreographed, notably the sinister *Before,
during, and after the Party.*

Although a number of things got moving in the
United States in the thirties—such as Balanchine's
American Ballet (later to become New York City
Ballet) and modern dance groups started by
pioneers such as Ruth St. Denis, Ted Shawn,
Martha Graham and others—it was not until the
war years that the great American dance explosion
really happened. By 1941 there were three major
classical companies virtually carrying on the
Diaghilev tradition. In addition to Ballet Russe de
Monte Carlo, based in the States since 1939, there
were two companies actually formed in America:
the forementioned American Ballet, and Ballet
Theatre (later American Ballet Theatre) formed in
1941. Four Russian painters, two of whom had
worked for Diaghilev, dominated design in those
formative years—Pavel Tchelitchev, Mstislav
Doboujinsky, Eugene Berman, and Marc Chagall.
All of Tchelitchev's ballet design in America was
for works by Balanchine. That same poetic sense,
totally at one with all the other creative elements,
which made his design of *Ode* for Diaghilev so
outstanding, was developed even further in
*Orpheus and Eurydice* (American Ballet, 1936),
*Balustrade* (de Basil's Ballets Russes, 1941),
*Apollon musagète* and *Concerto* (Teatro Colon,
Buenos Aires, 1942). Tchelitchev designed very
little for ballet but he stands out as one of the key
figures of theatre design in the twentieth century.
Eugene Berman had a colour sensitivity rather
similar to Tchelitchev's. Many of his designs
evoked the architectural perspective of the Italian
Renaissance; this was apparent in his work for
Balanchine's *Concerto Barocco* (American Ballet
Caravan, 1941) and—undoubtedly his
masterpiece—Antony Tudor's *Romeo and Juliet*
(Ballet Theatre, 1943). Doboujinsky, who
designed Fokine's *Papillons* for Diaghilev in 1914
and many classics for other European companies
after that, remained strictly in the early Russian
school influenced by Benois; he designed a
number of Ballet Theatre's early works, his most
important, however, being the first production of

29: CHRISTIAN BERARD: *La Rencontre* (Caron as Sphinx, Babilée as Oedipus);
music, Sauguet; chor., Lichine; given by Ballets des Champs-Elysées at Théâtre des
Champs-Elysées, Paris, 1948. (Photo: Lipnitzky)

Balanchine's *Ballet Imperial* (American Ballet,
1941). Chagall's designs had the rich glow of
Russian peasant art which earlier in the century
had inspired Goncharova and Larionov; his most
notable design was for Massine's *Aleko* (Ballet
Theatre, 1942) and for Bolm's version of *The
Firebird* (Ballet Theatre, 1945; same designs for
Balanchine's version for New York City Ballet,
given in 1949).

In the work of these four painters it could
hardly be said that anything was indigenous to the
American scene; in 1942, however, Agnes de Mille
created *Rodeo* for Ballet Russe de Monte-Carlo,
evoking the very air and loneliness of America's
wide open spaces, all of which was reflected in the
designs of Oliver Smith. He went on to design
what must be considered the first 'Americana'
ballets, notably Jerome Robbin's *Fancy Free*
(Ballet Theatre, 1944) and de Mille's *Fall River
Legend* (Ballet Theatre, 1948). But although these

30: LILA DI NOBILI: *Ondine* (act 2, prod. picture); music, Henze; chor., Ashton; given by the Royal Ballet at the Royal Opera House, Covent Garden, 1958. (Photo: Roger Wood)

works were concerned with American subjects they were still conceived in the more traditional painter's form. One of the most important design elements to emerge in America came when the sculptor Isamu Noguchi started working with Martha Graham in 1934, at first on props for her dances, later on sets and dresses which became an integral part of the contemporary dance language that Graham was then evolving. Although born in America, Noguchi received most of his art training in Japan; this gave him that wonderful Japanese economy of line and form which worked perfectly for Graham's style of writing and the subjects she chose (usually pioneering America or ancient Greek myth). In *Appalachian Spring* a few strips of polished wood, related to the space around them, were all that was needed to suggest a dwelling on the prairie. Similarly, in other works, his abstract sculptures—whether in wood, bone, stone, or twisted metal—around or through which the

dancers could move, always evoked the mood, time or place that was intended. One extraordinary effect was a white silk gauze which dribbled down like an oily fog, for the blinded Orpheus's journey to the underworld in the Balanchine/Stravinsky *Orpheus* for New York City Ballet.

Because Noguchi's sets were three-dimensional, imaginative lighting became vital. The remarkable visual image in all Graham's works was largely due to that great pioneer lighting designer, Jean Rosenthal, the true successor to Appia. As well as working for Graham, Rosenthal collaborated with Balanchine, and with the inauguration of New York City Ballet in 1948 her lighting of Balanchine's many neo-classic ballets was so brilliant that any other form of setting became totally superfluous. She did, however, design a set, a white dance studio which had the effect of being reflected in a mirror, for Jerome Robbins's

*Afternoon of a Faun*. It could be said that Rosenthal—together with Nananne Porcher, Nicholas Cernovitch and others—were to give dance a whole new dimension. Largely due to their work, the lighting designer came to take a place of honour alongside ballet's other creative elements.

The modern dance techniques that in America were to become as important as classical ballet, gave greater scope for design to enter into new relationships with the performance. Rouben Ter-Arutunian, a designer of infinite variety, at one period appeared to be influenced by Noguchi, in that for some works by Glen Tetley he used sculptural images which became an integral part of the dance: a shell-like winged structure in which a couple worked out their emotions for *Ricercare* ; or a simple quadrangular scaffolding as Pierrot's domain, and in which he could swing, for *Pierrot lunaire*. Then Merce Cunningham, like Tetley a former dancer with Martha Graham, involved the painter more positively than ever before; Robert Rauchenburg designed many of his works, notably a shimmering pointilliste set for *Summerspace*, but in some works Rauchenberg actually painted on stage and became a part of the dance as it was in progress. Cunningham employed the foremost modern painters and sculptors—such as Marcel Duchamp, Jasper Johns, Andy Warhol and so on—and their work became an organic part of

31: EUGENE BERMAN:
*Romeo and Juliet*
(set); music, Delius;
chor., Tudor; given
by Ballet Theatre at
Metropolitan Opera
House, New York, 1942.

Cunningham's conception. Possibly the most extraordinary example of media interrelationship came in the single person of Alwin Nikolais who himself choreographed, composed, designed, and lit his many works, to form a dramatic interaction of time, motion, space, sound, colour and light.

Such a fusion of elements could be seen as the climax to five centuries of ballet design, and the stepping stone towards even further interaction among the arts. Yet, for all it owes to complex modern technology, ballet design today continues to derive inspiration from the noble lineage stretching back to a Tortona banquet in the fifteenth century.

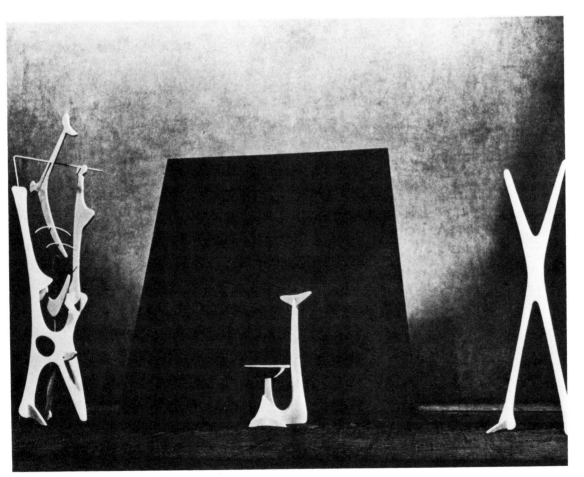

32: ISAMU NOGUCHI:
*Herodiad* (set model);
music, Hindemith;
chor., Graham; first given
by the Martha Graham
Dance Company
at the Library of
Congress, Washington,
D.C., 1944. (Photo:
Arnold Eagle)

33: ISAMU NOGUCHI:
*Seraphic Dialogue*
(prod. picture); music,
Dello Joio; lighting,
Rosenthal; chor.,
Graham; first given by
the Martha Graham
Dance Company at
ANTA Theatre,
New York, 1955.
(Photo: Bill Lewis)

34: JEAN ROSENTHAL:
*Afternoon of a Faun*
(Curley and Norman in
Ballet USA's prod.);
music, Debussy; chor.,
Robbins; first given by
the New York City
Ballet at City Center,
New York, 1953.

35: ALEXANDRE BENOIS: *Le Pavillon d'Armide*
(set, scene 2); book and design, Benois; music,
Tcherepnine; chor., Fokine; first given at the Maryinsky
Theatre, St. Petersburg, 25 November 1907.

This ballet first realized the reforms—about the
harmonious blending of music, painting and the plastic
arts—that Fokine and the *Mir Iskusstva* (*The World of
Art*) group had been working towards in St. Petersburg.
Benois based this scene, in which a tapestry comes to
life, on Versailles and the work of the seventeenth-
century landscape gardener, Le Nôtre.

34

36: ALEXANDRE BENOIS: *Petrushka* (set, scenes 1 and 4); book, Stravinsky and Benois; music, Stravinsky; design, Benois; chor., Fokine; first given by the Diaghilev Ballet at the Théâtre du Châtelet, Paris, 13 June 1911.

This ballet, a romantic tragedy about three puppets in a fair booth, is the first true masterpiece of the twentieth century in its perfect blending of the artistic elements.

Benois' design of this set (Admiralty Square during the St. Petersburg pre-Lenten carnival) and the two inset scenes, mixed the realism of the fairground and its jostling crowds with the symbolism of the story.

37: LÉON BAKST: *Schéhérazade:* book, Benois;
music, Rimsky-Korsakov; design, Bakst; chor., Fokine;
first given by the Diaghilev Ballet at the Théâtre
National de l'Opéra, Paris, 4 June 1911.

For this work, based on the first tale in *The Thousand
and One Nights,* Bakst made an intensive study of
Persian art, which he then translated into his own
dramatic terms. By contrasting brilliant colour masses
with darker recesses he evoked great sensuality. His
designs for this ballet were to have a profound effect on
interior decoration and fashion, especially on couturier
Paul Poiret, for many years to come.

38: LÉON BAKST: *Thamar* (set): book and design, Bakst; music, Balakirev; chor., Fokine; first given by the Diaghilev Ballet at the Théâtre du Châtelet, Paris, 20 May 1912.

Although, after its first seasons, *Thamar* never had the lasting success of *Schéhérazade*, Bakst's set is another example of the way he could evoke the nature, mood, and period of a particular work. His use of perspective brilliantly suggests a turret in the Georgian castle of Queen Thamar, to which she entices lovers by waving a scarf. Again Bakst's sense of form and dramatic use of colour reflects the cruelty and sensuality of the story.

39: LÉON BAKST: *The Sleeping Princess* (set, prologue or 'christening scene'); book (after Perrault) and chor., Petipa; music, Tchaikovsky; designs, Bakst; first given by the Diaghilev Ballet at the Alhambra Theatre, London, 2 November 1921.

Diaghilev, determined to bring the treasures of the Imperial Russian Ballet to the West, mounted this three-act Tchaikovsky/Petipa classic at a time when audiences had become accustomed to short contemporary works. Bakst very rightly sought inspiration from the architectural splendours of the Bibiena family, and his sets—in and around the palace of King Florestan XXIV—had a baroque opulence which set off dresses of great beauty and imagination. The revival, though an artistic triumph, was a financial disaster; later this set was salvaged and used for a *divertissement, Aurora's Wedding,* consisting of some of the principal dances from the ballet. Bakst's designs were to influence Oliver Messel when he designed *The Sleeping Beauty* for the Sadler's Wells Ballet in 1946.

40: NICHOLAS ROERICH: *Prince Igor* (set); music, Borodin; designs, Roerich; chor., Fokine; first given by the Diaghilev Ballet at the Théâtre du Châtelet, Paris, 18 May 1909.

The frenzied Polovtsians, in the dance scenes from Borodin's opera, sealed the success of Diaghilev's first Paris season. Roerich, whose painting had previously been seen in the Paris exhibitions of Russian art, brought all the loneliness and mystery of the steppes of primitive Russia to his set.

41: NATALIA GONCHAROVA: *Le Coq d'or* (scene
1); book (based on a poem by Pushkin), V. Bielsky,
revised by A. Benois; designs, Goncharova; chor.,
Fokine; Music, Rimsky-Korsakov; first given by the
Diaghilev Ballet at the Théâtre National de l'Opéra,
Paris, 21 May 1914.

Goncharova's first designing for Diaghilev was for the

opera/ballet version of Rimsky-Korsakov's opera; the
same designs, slightly modified, were used for a one-act
danced version for the de Basil company in 1937.
Inspired by Russian peasant art, Goncharova's brilliant
use of colour and form perfectly reflected the satirical
nature of Pushkin's fairytale.

42: NATALIA GONCHAROVA: *Les Noces*; words
and music, Stravinsky; designs, Goncharova; chor.,
Nijinska; first given at the Théâtre Gaîte-Lyrique, Paris,
13 June 1923.

Stravinsky finished his score in 1917; he had envisaged
that the work be given in traditional Russian dress.
When it was eventually performed the whole idea had
changed completely. Instead of using bright peasant
dresses, Goncharova designed the work with a starkness
that seemed totally right for the score; costumes of white
and earthy browns, against sets that were equally stark
and simple, worked perfectly with Nijinska's geometric
mass formations. The work remains a masterpiece in its
perfect integration of all the creative elements.

43: *Opposite:* MICHEL LARIONOV: *The Midnight
Sun* (costume for the Sun); music, Rimsky-Korsakov;
design, Larionov; chor., Massine; first given at the
Grand Theatre, Geneva, 20 December 1915.

This was the first work choreographed by Leonide
Massine to be seen by the public; it was also the first
ballet designed by the Russian painter, Larionov, who
also helped Massine in its creation. Larionov, like his
wife Goncharova, had been greatly influenced by the
peasant art of their native Russia. All this was reflected
in the bright colours and naïve forms that Larionov
brought to his design of the ballet, based on Rimsky-
Korsakov's opera *The Snow Maiden*.

44: PABLO PICASSO: *Le Tricorne* (set); book, Martinez Sierra; music, Manuel de Falla; design, Picasso; chor., Massine; first given by the Diaghilev Ballet at the Alhambra Theatre, London, 22 July 1919.

During 1917-18 the Diaghilev company was blocked in Spain, owing to wartime regulations; Diaghilev and Massine became so absorbed by the life and varied arts of that country that they were determined to make a ballet on a Spanish subject. Picasso, a native of Andalucia, was the obvious choice as designer. The Cubism of Picasso's first ballet (*Parade*, 1917) was less apparent in *Le Tricorne* although the houses (forming the stage wings) and most of the dresses were obviously inspired by this art form. The pale ochre backcloth, with a few lines to suggest distant buildings, brilliantly evoked the burning plains of Andalucia.

45: PABLO PICASSO: *Pulcinella* (set); music, Stravinsky; designs, Picasso; chor., Massine; first given by the Diaghilev Ballet at the Grand Opera, Paris, 15 May 1920.

Massine, during his early years in Italy, became deeply interested in the Commedia dell'Arte and decided to write a work based on one of the eighteenth-century scenarii. Picasso originally designed the ballet as a stage within a stage of a puppet theatre. This was discarded by Diaghilev, although later used for *Cuadro flamenco* in 1921. After several other projects had been rejected, Picasso's final version consisted of Cubistically treated houses in a backstreet, leading to the sea and a distant view of Vesuvius; the set brilliantly evokes the whole spirit of Naples in the simplest terms.

46: MARIE LAURENÇIN: *Les Biches* (frontcloth); music, Poulenc; design, Laurençin; chor., Nijinska; first given by the Diaghilev Ballet at the Théâtre de Monte-Carlo, 6 January 1924.

If any ballet can reflect social attitudes of a particular period, then *Les Biches* is the one that epitomizes the intellectual frivolity that existed during the twenties, in a world trying to forget the horrors of the 1914–18 war. All this was reflected in the work of the then fashionable painter, Laurençin. Diaghilev's choice of her to design this ballet, about the rather amoral goings-on at an elegant house party, was a brilliant one. The simple pastel dresses and set combine in a perfect evocation of the period.

47: ANDRÉ DERAIN: *La Boutique fantasque*
(backcloth); music, Rossini arr. Respighi; design,
Derain; chor., Massine; first given by the Diaghilev
Ballet at the Alhambra Theatre, London, 5 July 1919.

It was originally intended that Bakst should design this
ballet about dolls coming to life. But Diaghilev, then
absorbed by the School of Paris, discarded the idea in
favour of Derain. It was Derain's first work for the
theatre: his use of broad masses of clear colour, and the
sophisticated naïveté of his treatment, proved ideal for
the subject.

48: FERNAND LÉGER: *La Création du monde* (backcloth); book, Blaise Cendrars; music, Milhaud; design, Léger; chor., Borlin; first given by Les Ballets Suédois at the Théâtre des Champs-Elysées, Paris, 23 October 1923.

Even more avant-garde than Diaghilev in the twenties was the Ballets Suédois, formed by Rolf de Maré who engaged the foremost painters of the time. The Cubist painter Léger saw the creation of life on earth through the medium of African art. It was the first ballet to be so inspired, and led many later designers to seek inspiration from this source.

49: ANDRÉ DERAIN: *L'Épreuve d'amour* (backcloth); music, Mozart; design, Derain; chor., Fokine; first given by R. Blum's Ballet Russe de Monte-Carlo, 4 April 1936.

During the later part of his career, Fokine decided to make a ballet on a Mozart score that had recently been unearthed in Graz. He and Derain devised a story about the love of a mandarin's daughter for a poor Chinese fisherman; it worked perfectly with the nature of the eighteenth-century score. Derain's designs amounted to a modern painter's interpretation of chinoiserie, and the colours had the bright clarity of Oriental ceramics.

50: GEORGES ROUAULT: *Le Fils prodigue* (set, scene 2); book, Kochno; music, Prokofiev; designs, Rouault; chor., Balanchine; first given by the Diaghilev Ballet at the Théâtre Sarah Bernhardt, Paris, 20 May 1929.

This was to be the last creation for the Diaghilev Ballet.

The choice of Rouault, a modern painter who also designed stained-glass windows, was perfect for this biblical theme. The rather sombre sets had an incandescent glow which created exactly the right mood for the theme, choreography and score.

51: HENRI MATISSE: *L'Étrange Farandole*
(frontcloth); music, Shostakovich; design, Matisse;
chor., Massine; first given at the Théâtre de Monte-
Carlo, 11 May 1939 as *Rouge et noir*; at the
Metropolitan Opera House, New York, 28 October as
*L'Étrange Farandole*.

The great painter Matisse only designed two ballets. His
first, *Le Chant du rossignol* for Diaghilev in 1921, and
his second, *L'Étrange Farandole*, were both
choreographed by Massine. To the later work Matisse
brought his unerring sense of decorative values in
creating a background of abstract shapes and pure
colours, which were reflected in the dancers' tight-
fitting costumes.

52: CHRISTIAN BÉRARD: *Symphonie fantastique*
(scene 2); music, Berlioz; design, Bérard; chor.,
Massine; first given by de Basil's Ballet Russe at the
Royal Opera House, Covent Garden, 24 July 1936.

The Parisian painter Bérard was the most important
theatre designer in the immediate post-Diaghilev years.
His designing of *Symphonie fantastique* had a grandeur
of conception and dramatic use of form and colour that
perfectly complemented Berlioz' score and the theme,
concerning the fantasies in a poet's opium dream.

53: JOAN MIRÓ: *Jeux d'enfants*; book, Kochno; music, Bizet; designs, Miró; chor., Massine; first given by de Basil's Ballet Russe at the Théâtre de Monte-Carlo, 14 April 1932.

The Spanish painter, Miró, was the ideal choice to design this ballet about a child's dream of games and toys. The simple abstract set and the bright surrealist costumes, combined with Massine's choreography and the Bizet music, gave the impression of a nursery world seen through the mind of a child.

54: REX WHISTLER: *The Rake's Progress* (frontcloth and costumes for the Rake and Betrayed Girl); book and music, Gordon; design, Whistler; chor., de Valois; first given by the Vic-Wells Ballet at Sadler's Wells Theatre, London, 20 May 1935.

The ballet was based on Hogarth's series of paintings (bearing the same title as the ballet) and Whistler's designs brilliantly evoked the whole spirit of the paintings and of the seamier side of eighteenth-century London. Whistler had obviously been inspired by the form of Claud Lovat Fraser's famous designs for Nigel Playfair's production of *The Beggar's Opera*.

55: CECIL BEATON: *Apparitions* (set, scene 1); book, Lambert; music, Liszt; design, Beaton; chor., Ashton; first given by the Vic-Wells Ballet at the Sadler's Wells Theatre, London, 11 February 1936.

Like Massine's *Symphonie fantastique*, the story of *Apparitions* was about the fantasies of a poet's opium dream, graphically suggested by the gauzes in Beaton's sets. The dresses, seemingly inspired by Winterhalter, were of great elegance; the one for Fonteyn (as the Woman in the Ball-dress, centre of the design) was to start a fashion trend when couturier Victor Stiebel based a subsequent collection on it.

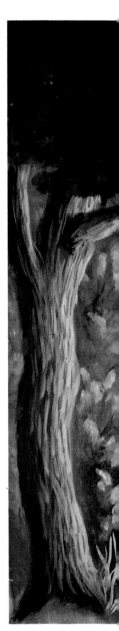

56: SOPHIE FEDOROVITCH: *Symphonic Variations* (set); music, César Franck; design, Fedorovitch; chor., Ashton; first given by the Sadler's Wells Ballet at the Royal Opera House, Covent Garden, 24 April 1946.

Fedorovitch had designed Frederick Ashton's first ballet (*A Tragedy of Fashion*, 1926) and had been his principal collaborator since then. *Symphonic Variations* was their first creation for the company after the Royal Opera

House became its home. Both made magnificent use of the large stage: Ashton in the masterly way he choreographed for only six dancers, perfectly deployed in the area; Fedorovitch in the way she filled her space with fine calligraphic lines, on a greenish-yellow backcloth, which seemed to flow as an extension of the music and dance.

57: HUGH STEVENSON: *Lilac Garden* (backcloth); book and chor., Tudor; music, Chausson; design, Stevenson; first given by the Ballet Club (later Ballet Rambert) at the Mercury Theatre, London, 26 January 1936.

Stevenson was one of several distinguished British designers to emerge from Marie Rambert's Ballet Club during the thirties. Most of his early work was for ballets by Antony Tudor, one of British ballet's pioneer choreographers, who later achieved greater international fame in America. In *Lilac Garden* Stevenson's designs evoked the bittersweet nature of a romantic garden, where lovers are temporarily reunited before being finally parted.

58: MARC CHAGALL: *The Firebird* (frontcloth);
music, Stravinsky; design, Chagall; chor., Balanchine;
first given by New York City Ballet at City Center,
New York, 29 November 1949.

Originally created for Diaghilev in 1910, when it first
revealed Stravinsky as a key figure in twentieth-century
music, *The Firebird* had an entirely new production by
Balanchine in America. The famous painter Chagall was
greatly inspired by East European folk art, as was
Goncharova in Diaghilev's time. His sets were in
sombre but glowing colours; his frontcloth is a brilliant
painting which immediately suggests to the audience the
half-avian, half-human nature of the legendary creature.

59: JOHN ARMSTRONG: *Façade* (backcloth); music, Walton; design, Armstrong; chor., Ashton; first given by the Camargo Society at the Cambridge Theatre, London, 26 April 1931.

Based on a series of poems by Edith Sitwell, set to music by William Walton, Ashton's *Façade* was—and remains—one of the wittiest ballets in the British repertory. It is a satire on various social and ethnic dance forms popular at the time. The painter John Armstrong heightened the comedy by his juxtaposition of realistic costumes with a set, in pale colour masses, which appeared to be the backyard of a Swiss chalet; it also contained certain references to the nature of the dances themselves.

58

60: LESLIE HURRY: *Hamlet* (set); music, Tchaikovsky; design, Hurry; chor., Helpmann; first given by the Sadler's Wells Ballet at the New Theatre, London, 19 May 1942.

Robert Helpmann, having admired an exhibition of Hurry's paintings, invited the painter to design *Hamlet*. The whole surrealist conception—incidents in Hamlet's tragedy seen through his dying moments—was brilliantly realized in Hurry's sense of Blake-like form and colour. After this, his first work for the theatre, Hurry went on to become one of Britain's leading stage designers.

61: JOHN PIPER: *The Quest* (set); music, Walton; design, Piper; chor., Ashton; first given by the Sadler's Wells Ballet at the New Theatre, London, 6 April 1943.

This was the first ballet to be designed by John Piper, a distinguished painter then famous for his romantic landscapes, frequently including neo-gothic buildings. His particular style was ideal for this ballet, based on Spenser's *The Faerie Queen*. Piper was later to design many notable ballets, mainly in collaboration with John Cranko.

62: OLIVER MESSEL: *Comus* (set); music, Purcell (arr. Lambert); design, Messel; chor., Helpmann; first given by the Sadler's Wells Ballet at the New Theatre, London, 14 January 1942.

Messel was Britain's foremost stage designer, principally for revues and musicals, during the thirties. His first ballet (Lichine's *Francesca da Rimini*, for de Basil's Ballet Russe, 1937) was a beautiful evocation of the Renaissance. Messel's sense of period and style was equally apparent in his work for Helpmann's first ballet, *Comus*, based on Milton's masque, which appeared to be inspired by English Restoration painters. It was Messel's first work for the Sadler's Wells Ballet and he was to design several more for the company, including the historic *Sleeping Beauty*.

63: SALVADOR DALI: *Bacchanale* (backcloth);
music, Wagner; design, Dali; chor., Massine; first given
by Ballet Russe de Monte Carlo at the Metropolitan
Opera House, New York, 9 November 1939.

This was the first ballet to be designed by the great
surrealist painter Salvador Dali, who suggested to
Massine the idea of a ballet based on the hallucinations
of Ludwig II of Bavaria, to Wagner's 'Venusberg' music
from *Tannhäuser*. The subject was ideally suited to
Dali's genius. Dali's set was dominated by a huge swan,
a symbol always associated with Ludwig, and the work
was full of hallucinatory surrealist images.

64: **EUGENE BERMAN**: *Danses concertantes*
(frontcloth); music, Stravinsky; design, Berman; chor.,
Balanchine; first given by Ballet Russe de Monte Carlo
at City Center, New York, 20 September 1944.

Berman was born in St. Petersburg, and as a child saw

many ballets at the Maryinsky Theatre. Later in Europe
he made a study of the Italian Renaissance and Baroque
masters. This had a great influence on his stage design
after he settled in America in 1937. His designing of
*Danses concertantes* shows these influences very clearly.

65: OLIVER SMITH: *Rodeo* (backcloth); music,
Copeland; set designs, Smith; chor., de Mille; first given
by Ballet Russe de Monte Carlo at the Metropolitan
Opera House, New York, 16 October 1942.

*Rodeo* was one of the first ballets for a classical company
to be based on a typical 'Americana' theme: life and
courtship on a ranch. Agnes de Mille's choreography
was based on American folklore (later developed by her
in the musical *Oklahoma*). Oliver Smith's sets, his first
for ballet, most graphically depicted the loneliness of the
open prairie, the land of the cowboy.

66: OLIVER SMITH: *Fancy Free* (set); music, Bernstein; set designs, Smith; chor., Robbins; first given by Ballet Theatre at the Metropolitan Opera House, New York, 18 April 1944.

*Fancy Free* was the first ballet to be choreographed by Jerome Robbins; it was so successful that he later adapted the theme—three sailors on shore leave in Manhattan—for the musical *On The Town*. Oliver Smith's set gave a vivid impression of a bar and New York street on a hot summer's night, where sailors might well pick up (or be picked up by) girls.

67: NICHOLAS GEORGIADIS: *House of Birds* (set); music, Mompou; design, Georgiadis; chor., MacMillan; first given by the Sadler's Wells Theatre Ballet at Sadler's Wells Theatre, 26 May 1955.

When Kenneth MacMillan was starting his career as a choreographer in the early fifties, he discovered Georgiadis, then a student at the Slade School of Art. From then on they were to work together on most of MacMillan's principal creations. *House of Birds*, their second collaboration, is a typical example of the way that Georgiadis uses his innate sense of form and colour to heighten the drama of a Bird Woman who turns young people into birds.

68: NICHOLAS GEORGIADIS: *Romeo and Juliet*
(set, final Tomb scene); music, Prokofiev; design,
Georgiadis; chor., MacMillan; first given by the Royal
Ballet at the Royal Opera House, Covent Garden, 9
February 1965.

This was the first three-act ballet from MacMillan, and
also from Georgiadis whose sense of colour and form,
mainly influenced by Mediterranean antiquity, created
exactly the right atmosphere of grandeur in the palaces,
squalor in the streets, of Renaissance Verona.

69: ANTONI CLAVÉ: *Carmen* (set, scene 2, at Lillas Pastia); music, Bizet; design, Clavé; chor., Petit; first given by Ballets de Paris at Prince's Theatre, London, 21 February 1949.

The Spanish painter Clavé was the ideal choice for Roland Petit's version of *Carmen*; his designs graphically evoked all the heat and squalor of Prosper Merimee's Seville. Clavé's use of vibrant colour and form, in which practical objects were assembled in perfect relationship with near-abstract sets, created a visual excitement seldom realized in the theatre since the early days of Léon Bakst.

70: JEAN CARZOU: *Le Loup*; book, Anouilh; music, Dutilleux; design, Carzou; first given at the Théâtre de l'Empire, Paris, 17 March 1953.

Anouilh's strange and rather brutal fantasy, about a young bride tricked into marrying a wolf, takes place in a forest. Unlike most designers who usually depict woodland scenes in soft curves, Carzou's forest consists of a perspective of stark and slender, very vertical, trees surmounted by a spiky filigree of entwined branches. It amounted to contemporary Romanticism, which perfectly reflected the nature of the theme and Petit's choreography.

71: LÉONOR FINI: *Les Demoiselles de la nuit* (set, scene 1, the home of Agathe); book, Anouilh; music, Françaix; design, Fini; chor., Petit; first given by Ballets de Paris at the Théâtre Marigny, Paris, 22 May 1948.

Anouilh's libretto, like his one for Petit's *Le Loup*, was concerned with the love of humans for transformed animals; in this case a cat, Agathe (a role created for Margot Fonteyn). Italian painter Léonor Fini heightened the air of poetic fantasy with her use of muted colour; she created an unusual effect by covering the walls of a room, where the cats lived, with sheets of newspaper.

72: JEAN HUGO: *Les Amours de Jupiter* (set, scene 1,
Europa and Taurus); book, Kochno; music, Ibert;
design, Hugo; chor., Petit; first given by Les Ballets de
Champs-Elysées at the Théâtre des Champs-Elysées,
Paris, 5 March 1946.

Jean Hugo's gouache paintings, usually of landscapes or
architecture in simple washes of clean opaque colours
with all detail eliminated, evoke the primitives. He
applies this same technique to his very distinguished
designing in the theatre, for drama and ballet. In Petit's
*Les Amours de Jupiter*, during which Jupiter in various
disguises (as a bull, a swan, a shower of gold, an eagle)
seduces the mortals he desires, Hugo managed to create
a wonderful feeling of Aegean sunlight and antiquity.

73: PETER FARMER: *Stages* (set); music,
Nordheim/Downes; design, Farmer; chor., Cohan; first
given by London Contemporary Dance Theatre at The
Place, London, 21 April 1971.

Robert Cohan's *Stages* was a modern Orphic myth, in
contemporary dance terms, about the descent of a hero
into an underworld in which the tortures of the damned
are seen in a 'Pop Art' image. Peter Farmer, a designer
more often associated with Romantic classics, created
many stunning and beautiful effects; use of three stage
levels added a new dimension to dance. This full-evening
multi-media work was responsible for bringing a new
audience, mainly of young people, to contemporary
dance during the company's tours of Britain and
Europe.

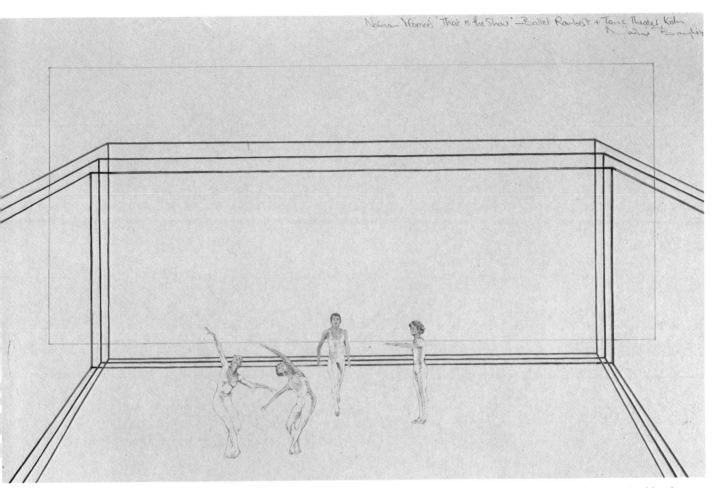

*Norman Morrice's "That is the Show" — Ballet Rambert + Tanz Theater Köln Nadine Baylis*

75: NADINE BAYLIS: *That is the Show* (set); music, Berio; design, Baylis; lighting, J. B. Read; chor., Morrice; first given by Ballet Rambert at the Jeannetta Cochrane Theatre, London, 6 May 1971.

Baylis, one of England's foremost designers, especially for contemporary dance works, creates dynamic spaces that, with the occasional addition of sculptural forms, evoke just the right atmosphere a particular work might need. In Morrice's *That is the Show*, inspired by the words and music in the five movements of Berio's *Sinfonia*, Baylis created a set—white with a few lines—suggesting a stage within a stage; with the dancers in white leotards and John B. Read's imaginative lighting, the work had a dreamlike quality which was perfect for the mood of the music and choreography.

74 *Opposite*: ROBERT RAUSCHENBURG: *Summerspace* (production picture); music, Feldman; design, Rauschenburg; chor., Cunningham; first given by the Merce Cunningham Dance Company at Connecticut College, New London, 17 August 1958. (Photo: Fred Fehl)

Merce Cunningham, a key figure in American contemporary dance, has used many of the foremost modern painters and sculptors in his creations; occasionally they have even been involved in the performance. Robert Rauschenburg, for example, has painted on the set and become an integral part of the dance itself. This was not the case, however, with *Summerspace* which Cunningham has called 'a lyric dance'; for this, Rauschenburg designed a shimmering pointillist landscape with the costumes treated in the same manner.

76: PETER DOCHERTY: *Ephemeron* (set); music, Milhaud; design, Docherty; chor., Darrell; first given by Western Theatre Ballet at Sadler's Wells Theatre, London, 20 June 1968.

Docherty was just finishing his student years at the stage design department of the Slade School when he designed his first ballet. The theme of *Ephemeron* is almost Proustian: a man's chance encounter with a girl he thought he knew, sets up a string of remembrances of things past. Docherty's black and malachite green textured space and shaded pink dresses were redolent of the twenties, the period of Darius Milhaud's score. An important aspect of Docherty's designing of this and his many subsequent and very successful ballets, has been his understanding of the nature and period of the music.

77 *Opposite*: ALWIN NIKOLAIS: *Tribe*, given at the Louis-Nikolais Dance Theatre Lab, New York, 1974; sound, choreography, design, lighting, all by Nikolais.

Through his work as director of the Henry Street Playhouse, Nikolais developed a form of total theatre in which dancers, sound, props and light became totally integrated in the whole conception. His works, which he describes as 'sound and vision pieces', become an abstract interaction of motion/dance, space exploration, synthesized sounds, light projection and props, all of which become an extension of the dance. In this way Nikolais brings dramatic meaning to the varied subjects of his works, of which *Tribe* is typical.

78: PATRICK PROCKTOR: *Cage of God*
(frontcloth); music, Rawsthorne; design, Procktor;
chor., J. Carter; first given by Western Theatre Ballet at
Sadler's Wells Theatre, 20 June 1967.

Many of the larger canvases of Patrick Procktor (one of several important British artists to come from the Slade School) are of figures in an enclosed landscape. This made him the ideal choice to design Jack Carter's *Cage of God* in which Adam, Eve and family are imprisoned forever as retribution for Original Sin. It was Procktor's first work for ballet, and this use of an easel painter in such a theatrical way recalled the last period of the Diaghilev Ballet.

79: TOER VAN SCHAYK: *Monument for a Dead Boy* (set); music, Boerman; design, van Schayk; chor., van Dantzig; first given by the Dutch National Ballet at the Stadsschouwburg, Amsterdam, 19 June 1965.

Toer van Schayk trained as a dancer but left that profession for six years to study art, with the result that he became a very successful painter and sculptor in Holland. He returned to dance, creating the principal role in Rudi van Dantzig's *Monument for a Dead Boy*, which also marked his debut as a stage designer. The work amounts to a psychological study taking place in the mind of a dying boy as he looks back on events caused by an unhappy family life, leading to his emotional confusion. All of this is reflected in van Schayk's abstract and suitably turgid designs.